Paul's SAT®
Practice Test 1

Paul Academy

SAT 집중공략 실전문제집!

Part 1_ 2016 Redesigned SAT 소개
Part 2_ Paul's SAT Practice Test #1
Part 3_ Paul's SAT Practice Test #1 정답 및 해설

SAT® is a registered trademark of the College Board, which is not affiliated with and does not endorse this product.

Contributors

Written and edited by the talented test prep professionals at
✓ Paul Academy

PaulAcademy is the publishing arm of one of the industry-leading test prep organizations in Asia. PaulAcademy is a dedicated test prep organization that has helped thousands of students to realize their potentials and achieve their dreams. As a leader in test prep & strategy development specializing in SAT, ACT and AP preparation, PaulAcademy teaches pragmatic problem-solving skills that will ultimately help students obtain successful academic results. PaulAcademy aims to spread the expert knowledge to students worldwide.

Editor-in-Chief
Paul Kim

Head of Publishing
Andrew Park

Material Development & Editing
Andy Kim, Kiara Kim, Hailey Sung, Esther Ra, Bryan Han

Marketing
Stephen Kim, Paul Jaewoo Jung

Email: books@paulacademy.net   Website: http://www.paulacademy.net

Copyright © 2015 All rights reserved by PaulAcademy.
The contents of the book may not be copied or reused without the expressed written consent of PaulAcademy.

"SAT" and "The Official SAT Study Guide" is a trademark of CollegeBoard, which is not affiliated with PaulAcademy. CollegeBoard does not endorse this product.

ISBN: 979-11-86461-05-1

Paul's SAT
Practice Test 1

Paul Academy

Paul's SAT Practice Test 1 서문

10여 년 전 "한국의 Test Prep이 세계 최고"라는 가능성을 보고 유학길에 올라 공부를 마치고 귀국 후 강남의 모 SAT 학원 팀장으로 매년 20%씩 성장을 이룬 후, 그 학원을 나와서 '친절한 폴샘'의 SAT 서문을 쓴 지도 이제 2년이 지났다. 그 당시에는 "아마존 Test Prep 분야 넘버원"이라는 꿈을 위해서 한국의 SAT 교재 1등을 달성한 후에 미국에 진출하고 싶다"고 이야기했는데, 그 2년 간 수많은 동역자들의 도움으로 한국 SAT 교재 베스트셀러(교보문고 기준)를 달성했고, 미국 Amazon.com에 진출하여 SAT Grammar 분야 4위, SAT Math 분야 15위를 기록했다. (2015년 5월 25일 기준) 글로벌 시장 진출을 위해서 시리즈 제목도 '친절한 폴샘의 SAT' 시리즈에서 'Paul's SAT', 'Paul's ACT' 시리즈로 정비하고 본격적인 미국 진출에 박차를 가하고 있다.

저자의 고교 시절에는 교과서, 학교 수업과 참고서만으로도 충분히 자기주도학습이 가능했지만, 지금은 학원에서 공부하지 않으면 효율적인 학습과 시험준비가 불가능하다는 견해가 이 사회에 팽배해 있는 것 같다. 저자는 좋은 교재와 콘텐츠를 만들어 사교육에 의존하지 않고도 자기주도학습이 가능하다는 것을 증명하고, 학습에 대한 잘못된 사회인식을 바로잡고, 더 나아가 미국 아마존의 Test Prep 분야에서 세계최고가 되어 '교육한류'의 한 축이 되고 싶다.

만일 누군가 독학이 힘들어 학원의 도움이 필요하다면, 폴아카데미에서 도움을 받기를 바란다. 폴아카데미에서는 본 교재를 사용하여 학생들이 빠른 시간 내에 고득점을 받을 수 있도록 도와주고, 혼자서 해결하기 힘든 부분들에 대한 해결책을 제시해 주고 있다.

이 책은 2015년 3월부터 새롭게 시행되는 "2016 Redesigned SAT"를 대비할 수 있도록 문제지와 정답, 그리고 간결하고 강력한 해설을 제공하는 실전문제집이다. 그 첫 번째 시리즈로서 우선 출간된 TEST 1에는 풀테스트 1세트가 실려있으며, 정답 및 해설이 같이 제공되어 스스로 틀린 부분을 점검하고 강화할 수 있다.

본 교재와 콘텐츠를 통해 단기간에 고득점을 가능하게 하고, 그렇게 확보된 소중한 시간을 본인이 진정으로 하고 싶은 것을 하면서 사는 세상을 만드는데 기여하는데 이 책이 좋은 첫걸음이 되길 바란다. "Paul's SAT Practice Test"가 빛을 볼 수 있도록 많은 사람들이 도움을 주었다. 내게 "best place to work"의 꿈을 심어주신 하늘에 계신 사랑하는 아버지, 못난 아들을 위해 항상 기도해 주시는 사랑하는 어머니, 부족한 남편임에도 열심히 섬겨주는 사랑하는 아내, 그리고 바쁘다는 이유로 함께 시간을 갖지 못해도 바르게 자라주고 있는 사랑하는 두 아들 영준, 경준에게 너무나 고맙고 사랑한다는 말을 전하고 싶다. 마지막으로 길가의 돌멩이보다 못한 나에게 비전을 주시고 여건을 허락해 주신 하나님께 감사를 드린다.

Paul Kim

NYU에서 영어교육을 전공하였으며 실력 있는 SAT, ACT 부문 최고의 전문강사로서 세한아카데미에서 수많은 학생을 가르치며 큰 명성을 쌓아온 Paul Kim은 현재 Test Prep 전문기관 Paul Academy의 대표로 재직하고 있다. Paul Academy에서는 SAT 및 ACT 교재 시리즈 출간, 온라인 교육 콘텐츠 개발, 자기주도학습과 수험생을 위한 영어교육 전반에 힘을 쏟고 있다.

CONTENTS

Part 1_ 2016 Redesigned SAT 소개 ················· 7

Part 2_ Paul's SAT Practice Test #1 ················· 15
    Section 1. Reading Test ················· 18
    Section 2. Writing & Language Test ················· 34
    Section 3. Math Test (No Calculator) ················· 50
    Section 4. Math Test (Calculator) ················· 58

Part 3_ Paul's SAT Practice Test # 1 정답 및 해설 ··········· 75

Part 4_ Scoring Your SAT Practice Test 1 ················· 123

Part 1

2016 Redesigned SAT 소개

SAT 시험, 이렇게 바뀐다!

2016 Redesigned SAT 소개

시행일시 : 2016년 3월부터 시행될 예정

1. Redesigned SAT 주요변화

A. 점수
- 전체 2,400점 만점 → 1,600점 만점 (Reading + Writing & Language 800점, Math 800점)
- 에세이는 선택사항으로 변경되고 점수도 독자적으로 매겨진다. Reading, analysis, writing 각 항목에 대해서 2~8점 배점되고 총점은 24점
- 에세이가 선택사항으로 바뀌었지만 상위권 대학을 희망하는 학생들은 필수적으로 점수를 받아놓아야 한다.

B. 영역
Essay, Critical Reading, Writing, Math 였던 영역구분이
→ Evidence-based Reading & Writing(Reading + Writing & Language), Math, Essay(선택사항) 으로 변경됨

C. 시험시간

전체 3시간 45분이었던 것이 3시간으로 축소. (에세이를 선택할 경우에는 3시간 50분)

1. Evidence-based Reading & Writing: Reading 65분, Writing 35분

2. Math: 55분 계산기 허용, 25분 계산기 사용불가

D. 시험 문제수
- Critical Reading: 67문제 → 52문제
- Writing: 49문제 → 44문제
- Essay: 1문제 그대로
- Math: 54문제 → 58문제

E. 시험 출제방식
- 오지선다에서 사지선다 방식으로 변경
- 지필시험방식을 유지

F. 채점방식 및 기준
- Essay: 글의 일관성보다는 학생의 분석능력과 논증과정을 중시
- 오답에 대한 감점제도 폐지: 틀린 문제와 풀지 않은 문제가 성적에 영향을 주지 않음

G. 기존 SAT와 새로운 SAT 비교표

현재 SAT			2016 Redesigned SAT			
과목	시험시간	문제 수	과목	시험시간	문제 수	시험방식
Critical Reading	70분	67문제	Reading	65분	52문제	4 LP 1 DP
Writing	60분	49문제	Writing & Language	35분	44문제	4 Passages
Essay	25분	1문제	Essay	50분	1문제	1 EP 1 RP
Math	70분	54문제	Math	80분	58문제	계산기/ 38문제 NO계산기/ 20문제
계	225분	171문제	계	180분 (에세이 포함시 230분)	154문제 (에세이 포함시 155문제)	

※참고 – LP: Long Passages, DP: Double Passages, EP: Essay Prompt, RP: Reading Passage

2. 과목별 구체적인 변화

A. Reading Test (독해)
1. 단어의 난이도 보다는 context에 집중
   - 기존의 단어 뜻 모르면 풀 수 없는 obscure한 문제 폐지
   - Extended context에서 단어 톤 찾기
     예) how word choice shapes tone/impact
   - Sentence Completion 폐지
   - 단편적인 정보, 직접적으로 단어 뜻을 물어보는 문제는 축소

2. Analysis & evidence use (분석, 근거 사용)
   - 답을 찾아내는 것뿐 아니라 텍스트의 어느 부분이 그 답을 support하는지 찾아야 한다
     예) Which portion of the passage best supports the answer to the text?
     CB: "There will be at least one question asking them to select a quote from the text that best supports the answer they have chosen in response to the preceding question."

3. Real-world에 관한 지문

- 기존의 임의적인 토픽의 essay와 fiction은 나오지 않음
- 차트, 그래프, 인포그래픽이 포함된 지문 (reading, writing, math 모두 동일하게 적용됨)
- 1개의 역사/사회 지문과 1개의 과학지문

4. 새로운 지문

> **학습전략**
>
> 2016 Revised SAT는 Evidence-based reading을 강조하므로 글의 paragraph summary, main idea, tone을 꼼꼼히 체크해가면서 글을 읽고 이해를 하며, 리딩문제를 풀 때 더 이상 '감'에 의존해서 푸는 것이 아니라 몇 번째 line을 통해서 답을 유추했는지를 항상 확인하면서 공부를 해야 한다. 혼자 하기 어려운 학생은 친절한 폴샘의 기출해설서의 CR 영역을 공부하면 된다.
>
> ### Passage Reading Q6-24
>
> #### Short passage 1 Q6-7
>
> *Passage Summary*
> **Ln. 1-14** author looks up at the stars and a comet, while horses don't look up at all, which makes him/her feel good to be human (since only humans look up and philosophize about these things)
>
> *Tone* : happy, appreciative "wonderous" (line 10) "good" (line 12)
>
> *Vocabulary and Phrases*
> **Ln. 1** Whistling and moaning 휫바람 불듯 그리고 불평하듯 (바람이) whipped: (채찍을 하듯) 불었다.
> **Ln. 3** slid a river of clouds that … all day(line4) 엄청난 구름이 오르락 내리락 하는 모습 설명.
> **Ln. 5** Comet hale-Bopp hung like … the punishing wind (line7) 혜성 Hale-Bopp이 깃털로 만든 낚시의 미끼처럼 하늘에 떠있었다. 그 혜성의 꼬리 부분은 바람한테 벌을 받아 밀려 약간 휘어있었다. 석양이 지면 회색으로 변하는 구름들이 이뤄진 강이 유유이 흘러간다. 구름이 오르락 내리락했다.
> **Ln. 5** lure   n. 매력
> **Ln. 9** gossamer   n. 아주 가는 거미줄
> swath   n. 면봉, 봉
> spectacle   n. 구경거리
>
> **6. THING: Contrasting Pair (Animal vs. Human perception)**
> *Answer key*: 이 질문은 "What can humans do that horses can't?"로 바꾸어 생각할 수 있다. "gossamer swath of Hale-Bopp" (line 9), "wondrous spectacle that is the night sky" (line 10) 에서 볼 수 있듯이 author는 자연의 아름다움을 묘사하고 있다. (D)에서만 "nature's beauty"를 mention함으로 (D)가 답이다.
>
> **Key point** Hale-Bopp, night sky = nature's beauty
>
> *Eliminate*
> (A) mistake는 not mentioned
> (B) company of others는 not mentioned
> (C) past experiences는 not mentioned
> (E) simplicity는 not mentioned
>
> 특별히 CR이 600점대 이하의, 유학 3년차 이하의 학생들은 찍기 식으로 가르치는 학원보다는 지문을 잘 이해시켜 주는 curriculum을 제공하는 학원과 교재를 선정하여 공부하는 것이 좋다. 그리고 SAT는 미국대학에 진학하려는 학생을 위한 시험이므로, 평소에 미국적 사고에 필요한 역사, 문학, 사회이슈들에 대한 배경지식을 잘 정리해 놓으면 지문을 이해하고 문제풀이 시간을 줄이는데 도움이 된다.

B. Writing and Language Test (문법)

1. Real-world에 관한 지문
   - 역사/사회, 과학, 인문학, Career 관련 지문
   - 그래프, 도표 문제 한 개 이상 출제: 주어진 정보들을 어떻게 잘 연결해서 자연스럽고 논리적인 글로 만들어낼 수 있는가에 대한 문제 출제

2. 문법적 오류 관련문제는 크게 변화 없음
   - Development of idea
     예) adding relevant supporting details, improving focus and cohesion
   - Careful & purposeful use of words
     예) improving precision or concision
   - Rhetoricals and conventions
     예) fragments & run-ons, parallel structure, modifier, tense, pronoun & number, verb agreement, logical comparison, idiom, punctuation
   - Diction

3. 주어진 텍스트와 차트 또는 도표 간의 연관 찾기
   예) 차트에 대한 잘못된 해석 고치기

4. 지문 길이 증가
   - 기존의 한 문장 짜리 문법 문제 폐지
   - Extended context를 제공하는 문단 제공

> **학습전략**
>
> 기존 SAT Grammar 섹션에서 나오는 Improving Paragraph 유형에 Grammar 요소가 조금 더 가미되었다고 보면 된다. 너무 걱정하지 말고 조만간 출간될 Paul' SAT Writing and Language로 준비하면 된다. 아직 교재가 출간되지 않아 조바심이 나는 경우는 친절한 폴샘의 SAT Grammar 기본서로 공부를 해도 대부분 커버할 수 있으니 너무 걱정하지 말자.

C. Essay (에세이)

1. 요구사항에서 선택사항으로 변경

2. 짧게 자신의 의견을 요구하는 prompt 폐지
   - 기존의 prompt는 배경지식과 경험에 의존; 논리구조만 맞으면 fact는 상관 없었지만 새로운 SAT Essay 에서는 600~700 단어로 주어진 글을 읽고 그 주장을 분석해서 설명해야 함 → 자기 마음대로 예시를 쓰거나, 단순히 자신의 주장을 펼치는 것이 아니라는 점에 주의
     예) 작가가 어떻게 주장을 이끌어 나가는지 텍스트 속 객관적 근거를 제시하여 설명하여야 하며, 자신의 의견은 쓰지 않음
   - 글쓴이의 주장과 논리를 분석하여 그 논리전개에 대하여, 또한 그 주장에 대한 찬성 또는 반대의 관점을 어떻게 자기의 말로 잘 풀어내는지가 포인트

3. 채점방식 및 기준

- 기존의 0~12점대의 scale은 폐지되고 criteria에 따른 점수로 0~24점까지 채점
- Reading: Source text와 main idea에 대한 이해가 중요하며, 얼마나 디테일이 정확한지, 텍스트 속의 근거를 얼마나 잘 사용하는지 등이 중요한 포인트
- Analysis: 주어진 과제를 얼마나 잘 이해했는지, 작가가 논거를 펼치며 사용한 각종 element가 얼마나 효과적인지, 그리고 자신의 주장에 대한 근거를 잘 제시하고 있는지 부분에 중점
- Writing: Central claim 사용, 효과적인 organization과 progression이 되고 있는지, 문장구조가 varied한지, 정확한 뜻의 단어를 사용하는지, 그리고 consistent한 스타일과 톤을 유지하는지, 문법적인 오류는 없는지 등이 중점채점사항

4. 에세이 시간이 25분에서 50분으로 길어졌기 때문에, 체계적인 논리와 전개과정이 필수적이다. 시간이 길어지면서 그만큼 평가도 정확하고 가혹하게 될 것이라 예상된다.

학습전략

기존 SAT는 내용을 '지어낼' 수 있었던 반면, Redesigned SAT는 fact-based essay이다. 2016 Redesigned Reading처럼 저자의 main idea와 argument를 잘 파악하여 fact-based argument를 하는 연습이 매우 중요해졌다. 이 연습만 잘 된다면 해외고 유학생들이 국내대학의 영어특기자 입시를 준비할 경우에 많은 도움이 될 것이다.

D. Math Test (수학)

출제범위 및 비중이 조정되었기 때문에 일단 전반적으로 수학문제의 난이도가 올라가게 되며, 일부 문제는 AP 시험유형과 수준의 문제라고 생각하고 준비해야 한다.

1. Data Analysis에 중점
   - Reading과 Writing에서 Real-world에 중점을 둔 것과 같은 맥락
   - 실제 상황에 적용해서 푸는 문제들이 출제된다는 뜻

2. Real-world context 사용한 문제 출제
   예) 사회/역사/과학과 관련된 시나리오를 보여준 후 그것에 대한 문제 여러 개 출제

3. Pre-Calculus 영역이 추가됨
   - Trigonometry, Complex Number, Radians 등의 상급개념 추가

4. 일부 섹션에서 계산기 사용이 제한됨
   - 복잡한 계산은 아니고 유리수 산술계산 정도의 수준
   - Grid-ins 형태의 주관식이 총 12문제 출제

〈출제범위〉

범위	문제 개수	출제비중
Heart of Algebra (Creating, Solving, Interpreting Linear Expressions)	21	36%
Problem Solving and Data Analysis	16	27%
Passport to Advanced Math (Quadratic/Exponential Functions)	15	26%
Additional Topics (Area/Volume Calculation, Investigation of Lines, Angles, Triangles and Circles Using Theorem, Working with Trigonometric Functions)	6	11%
계	58	100%

〈계산기 사용에 따른 구분〉

구분	유형	시험시간
계산기 사용가능	객관식 30문제 Grid-ins 8문제	55분
계산기 사용불가	객관식 15문제 Grid-ins 5문제	25분
계	총 58문제	총 80분

> **학습전략**
>
> Pre-Calculus 영역을 중점 학습하고, 특히 trigonometry(삼각함수), complex number(복소수), radians(호도법) 등의 개념학습을 충실히 한다. 그리고 계산기를 사용할 수 없는 section이 하나 있으므로, 평소 계산연습을 많이 해 두도록 하고, real-world situation에 입각한 문제에 대비하기 위해 관련 응용문제 풀이를 많이 하도록 한다. 여름방학에 2016 SAT 학원수강을 하게 되면 꼭 꼭 Math수업을 수강하여서 고득점의 발판을 마련하여야 한다. 더 이상 SAT 1 Math는 유학생들에게 쉬운 과목이 아니라는 점을 꼭 명심하도록 하자.

Part 2

SAT® Practice Test #1

Test begins on the next page.

Reading Test

65 MINUTES, 52 QUESTIONS

Turn to Section 1 of your answer sheet to answer the questions in this section.

DIRECTIONS

Each passage or pair of passages below is followed by a number of questions. After reading each passage or pair, choose the best answer to each question based on what is stated or implied in the passage or passages and in any accompanying graphics (such as a table or graph).

Questions 1-10 are based on the following passage.

The following passage is an excerpt from *Anna Karenina* by Leo Tolstoy, 1877. Translated from Russian by Constance Garrett.

"Varenka Andreevna, when I was very young, I set before myself the ideal of the woman I loved and should be happy to call my wife. I have lived through a long life, and now for the first time I
[5] have met what I sought—in you. I love you, and offer you my hand."

Sergey Ivanovitch was saying this to himself while he was ten paces from Varenka. Kneeling down, with her hands over the mushrooms to
[10] guard them from Grisha, she was calling little Masha.

"Come here, little ones! There are so many!" she was saying in her sweet, deep voice.

Seeing Sergey Ivanovitch approaching, she did
[15] not get up and did not change her position, but everything told him that she felt his presence and was glad of it.

"Well, did you find some?" she asked from under the white kerchief, turning her handsome,
[20] gently smiling face to him.

"Not one," said Sergey Ivanovitch. "Did you?"

She did not answer, busy with the children who thronged about her.

"That one too, near the twig," she pointed out
[25] to little Masha a little fungus, split in half across its rosy cap by the dry grass from under which it thrust itself. Varenka got up while Masha picked the fungus, breaking it into two white halves. "This brings back my childhood," she added,
[30] moving apart from the children beside Sergey Ivanovitch.

They walked on for some steps in silence. Varenka saw that he wanted to speak; she guessed of what, and felt faint with joy and panic. They
[35] had walked so far away that no one could hear them now, but still he did not begin to speak. It would have been better for Varenka to be silent. After a silence it would have been easier for them to say what they wanted to say than after talking
[40] about mushrooms. But against her own will, as it were accidentally, Varenka said:

"So you found nothing? In the middle of the wood there are always fewer, though." Sergey Ivanovitch sighed and made no answer. He was
[45] annoyed that she had spoken about the mushrooms. He wanted to bring her back to the first words she had uttered about her childhood; but after a pause of some length, as though against his own will, he made an observation in
[50] response to her last words.

"I have heard that the white edible funguses are found principally at the edge of the wood, though I can't tell them apart."

Some minutes more passed, they moved still
55 further away from the children, and were quite alone. Varenka's heart throbbed so that she heard it beating, and felt that she was turning red and pale and red again.

To be the wife of a man like Koznishev, after
60 her position with Madame Stahl, was to her imagination the height of happiness. Besides, she was almost certain that she was in love with him. And this moment it would have to be decided. She felt frightened. She dreaded both his speaking
65 and his not speaking.

Now or never it must be said—that Sergey Ivanovitch felt too. Everything in the expression, the flushed cheeks and the downcast eyes of Varenka betrayed a painful suspense. Sergey
70 Ivanovitch saw it and felt sorry for her. He felt even that to say nothing now would be a slight to her. Rapidly in his own mind he ran over all the arguments in support of his decision. He even said over to himself the words in which he meant
75 to put his offer, but instead of those words, some utterly unexpected reflection that occurred to him made him ask:

"What is the difference between the 'birch' mushroom and the 'white' mushroom?"
80 Varenka's lips quivered with emotion as she answered:

"In the top part there is scarcely any difference, it's in the stalk."

And as soon as these words were uttered, both
85 he and she felt that it was over, that what was to have been said would not be said; and their emotion, which had up to then been continually growing more intense, began to subside.

"The birch mushroom's stalk suggests a dark
90 man's chin after two days without shaving," said Sergey Ivanovitch, speaking quite calmly now.

"Yes, that's true," answered Varenka smiling, and unconsciously the direction of their walk changed. They began to turn towards the
95 children. Varenka felt both sore and ashamed; at the same time she had a sense of relief.

When he had got home again and went over the whole subject, Sergey Ivanovitch thought his previous decision had been a mistaken one. He
100 could not be false to the memory of Marie.

1

The purpose of the first sentence of the passage is to
A) describe the speaker's indecisiveness.
B) show the relationship between two characters by introducing their initial conversation.
C) establish the speaker's motivation regarding another character.
D) contrast the speaker's words with his emotional state.

2

The passage indicates that when Sergey approaches Varenka, he views her as
A) a childhood friend.
B) an intimidating beauty.
C) a potential spouse.
D) a fellow nature enthusiast.

3

Which choice provides the best evidence for the answer to the previous question?
A) Lines 1-6 ("Varenka ... hand.")
B) Lines 18-20 ("Well ... him.")
C) Lines 46-50 ("He ... words.")
D) Lines 61-62 ("Besides ... him.")

4

According to the passage, Varenka's behavior toward Sergey is mainly caused by her

A) enthusiasm to advance to a higher social standing.
B) eager anticipation of intentions mixed with a lack of confidence.
C) reluctance toward the potential marriage but pleasure with his presence.
D) shameful acceptance of Sergey's affection mixed with joy.

5

The mushrooms that recur throughout the paragraph have primarily which effect?

A) They are used by the characters to avoid speaking of a momentous subject.
B) They evoke memories of childhood for the characters.
C) They directly cause the two characters feelings of powerlessness and embarrassment.
D) They reflect the longing of the characters to break free from social convention.

6

When Varenka makes a comment about the scarcity of mushrooms in the middle of the wood, her words mainly have the effect of

A) disrupting the flow of conversation by introducing an entirely new subject.
B) suggesting her uncertainty about how to respond to his proposal.
C) provoking Sergey's temper by touching on a delicate subject.
D) making it more difficult for Sergey to broach the topic on his mind.

7

Which choice provides the best evidence for the answer to the previous question?

A) Lines 36-40 ("It ... mushrooms.")
B) Lines 44-46 ("He ... mushrooms.")
C) Lines 56-58 ("Varenka's ... again.")
D) Lines 63-65 ("And ... speaking.")

8

The passage indicates that, after his walk with Varenka, Sergey decides that his original intention was

A) ill-planned and badly executed.
B) deluded in its assumptions.
C) tactless about the setting.
D) faithless to his past.

9

During the course of the passage, Varenka's feelings shift from

A) anticipation about a future change in position to acknowledgment of situational difficulties.
B) reflection on her childhood to anxiety over her future.
C) nervous excitement about a possible proposal to relief and shame over its failure.
D) admiration of Sergey to self-blame over a poorly-chosen comment.

10

Which of the following most effectively summarizes the passage?

A) The memory of his past detains a man from making a proposal of marriage.
B) Two characters drift from their original subject of conversation to a less interesting topic.
C) A woman experiences hope, then fear, and finally humiliation.
D) A character plans to make a proposal of marriage, but gives up when an irrelevant subject diverts him.

Question 11-20 are based on the following passage.

The following passage is an excerpt from Book 3 of *Meditations* by Marcus Aurelius, written in 167 AD, translated from Koine Greek by George Long in 1862.

Do not waste the remainder of your life in thoughts about others, or at least do so only when you refer your thoughts to some common goal.
Line For you lose the opportunity of doing something
5 else when you have such thoughts as these: what is such a person doing, and why, and what is he saying, and what is he thinking of, and what is he contriving, and whatever else of the kind which makes us wander away from the observation of
10 our own driving purpose.
    We ought then to check in the series of our thoughts everything that is without a purpose and useless, but most of all the over-curious feeling and the malignant. A man should use
15 himself to think only of those things which, if someone should suddenly ask "What are you thinking?", with perfect openness one can immediately answer "This or That", and from what you say it will be plain that everything about
20 you is simple and benevolent. This is what benefits a social animal, and you should appear to care not for thoughts about pleasure or sensual enjoyments at all, or have any rivalry or envy and suspicion, or anything else that would make you
25 blush if you said you were thinking about it.
    For the man who is like this, and no longer delays being among the number of the best, is like a priest and minister of the gods, using too the deity which is planted within him, which makes
30 the man uncontaminated by pleasure, unharmed by any pain, untouched by any insult, feeling no wrong, a fighter in the noblest fight, one who cannot be overpowered by any passion, dyed deep with justice, accepting with all his soul everything
35 which happens and is assigned to him as his portion; and not often, nor yet without great necessity and for the general interest, imagining what another says, or does, or thinks.
    For it is only what belongs to him that he uses
40 as a motivation; and he constantly thinks of that which has been allotted to himself out of the sum total of things, and he makes his own acts fair, and he is persuaded that his own portion is good. For the lot which is assigned to each man is
45 carried along with him and carries him along with it. And he remembers also that every rational animal is his brother, and that to care for all men is according to man's nature; and a man should hold on to the opinion not of all, but of those only
50 who attempt to live according to nature.
    But as to those who do not live so, this man always bears in mind what kind of men they are both at home and away from home, both by night and by day, and what they are, and with what men
55 they live an impure life. Accordingly, he does not value at all the praise which comes from such men, since they are not even satisfied with themselves.

11

The main problem Aurelius is concerned with is that men

A) are egoistic beings, caring only about themselves.
B) are discontent with their lives and hope to deviate from the banality of the everyday.
C) do not assert their own thoughts and beliefs, losing their purpose in life.
D) are corrupt and inhumane, enjoying secular and sensual pleasures.

12

As used in line 8, "contriving" most nearly means

A) creating.
B) inventing.
C) planning.
D) fabricating.

13

Aurelius uses the phrase "make you blush" (line 24-25) mainly to highlight what he sees as

A) delightful imagination.
B) thoughts shameful to oneself.
C) socially benevolent ideas.
D) ambiguous feelings.

14

As used in line 43, "portion" most nearly means

A) inheritance.
B) amount of food.
C) part of a whole.
D) fate.

15

Aurelius claims that which of the following is a human responsibility?

A) To support other reasonable people
B) To accept everyone's opinions regardless of who they are
C) To become spiritually enlightened
D) To strive for a single universal aspiration

16

Which choice provides the best evidence for the answer to the previous question?

A) Lines 1-3 ("Do not … goal.")
B) Lines 26-38 ("For the … thinks.")
C) Lines 46-50 ("And he … to nature.")
D) Lines 55-58 ("Accordingly … themselves.")

17

It can be reasonably inferred that Aurelius views the "men" (line 52) as

A) courageous men of principle who can lead their own lives.
B) average people who rarely strive for more than what they are allotted.
C) insecure beings who do not have their own thoughts and purpose in life.
D) distrustful men with malignant personalities.

18

Aurelius claims that if a person owns his own life and thoughts, he or she is

A) content with his life and makes the most out of it.
B) willing to go beyond what was given to him.
C) dissatisfied with the boundaries of his life.
D) able to develop any ideas or feelings without restriction.

19

Which choice provides the best evidence for the answer to the previous question?

A) Lines 5-10 ("What is … purpose.")
B) Lines 11-14 ("We ought … malignant.")
C) Lines 26-38 ("For the … thinks.")
D) Lines 39-46 ("For it is … it.")

20

The second paragraph (lines 11-25) is mostly concerned with setting a contrast between

A) appropriate thoughts and inappropriate thoughts.
B) rational people and irrational people.
C) benevolence and malevolence.
D) animals and humans.

Questions 21-31 are based on the following passage and supporting material.

The passage is based on *Hyperloop Alpha* by Elon Musk and SpaceX, 2013.

When the California "high speed" rail was approved, I was quite disappointed, as I know many others were too. How could it be that the
Line home of Silicon Valley and JPL—doing incredible
5 things like indexing all the world's knowledge and putting rovers on Mars—would build a bullet train that is both one of the most expensive per mile and one of the slowest in the world? The underlying motive for a statewide mass transit
10 system is a good one. It would be great to have an alternative to flying or driving, but obviously only if it is actually better than flying or driving. The train in question would be both slower, more expensive to operate (if unsubsidized) and less
15 safe by two orders of magnitude than flying, so why would anyone use it? If we are to make a massive investment in a new transportation system, then the return should by rights be equally massive. Compared to the alternatives, it
20 should ideally be: safer, faster, lower cost, more convenient, immune to weather, sustainably self-powering, resistant to earthquakes, and not disruptive to those along the route. Is there truly a new mode of transport? A fifth mode after
25 planes, trains, cars and boats—that meets those criteria and is practical to implement? As things stand today, there is not even a short distance demonstration system operating in test pilot mode anywhere in the world, let alone something
30 that is robust enough for public transit. They all possess, it would seem, one or more fatal flaws that prevent them from coming to fruition.

The Hyperloop (or something similar) is, in my opinion, the right solution for the specific
35 case of high traffic city pairs that are less than about 1500 km or 900 miles apart. Around that inflection point, I suspect that supersonic air travel ends up being faster and cheaper. With a high enough altitude and the right geometry, the
40 sonic boom noise on the ground would be no louder than current airliners, so that isn't a showstopper. Also, a quiet supersonic plane immediately solves every long distance city pair without the need for a vast new worldwide
45 infrastructure. However, for a sub several hundred mile journey, having a supersonic plane is rather pointless, as you would spend almost all your time slowly ascending and descending and very little time at cruise speed. In order to go fast, you
50 need to be at high altitude where the air density drops exponentially, as air at sea level becomes as thick as molasses (not literally, but you get the picture) as you approach sonic velocity.

So what is Hyperloop anyway? Short of
55 figuring out real teleportation, which would of course be awesome (someone please do this), the only option for super fast travel is to build a tube over or under the ground that contains a special environment. This is where things get tricky. At
60 one extreme of the potential solutions is some enlarged version of the old pneumatic tubes used to send mail and packages within and between buildings. You could, in principle, use very powerful fans to push air at high speed through a
65 tube and propel people-sized pods all the way from LA to San Francisco.

However, the friction of a 350 mile long column of air moving at anywhere near sonic velocity against the inside of the tube is so
70 stupendously high that this is impossible for all practical purposes. Another extreme is the approach, that of drawing a hard or near hard vacuum in the tube and then using an electromagnetic suspension. The problem with
75 this approach is that it is incredibly hard to maintain a near vacuum in a room, let alone 700

miles (round trip) of large tube with dozens of
station gateways and thousands of pods entering
and exiting every day. All it takes is one leaky seal
80 or a small crack somewhere in the hundreds of
miles of tube and the whole system stops
working. However, a low pressure (vs. almost no
pressure) system set to a level where standard
commercial pumps could easily overcome an air
85 leak and the transport pods could handle variable
air density would be inherently robust.

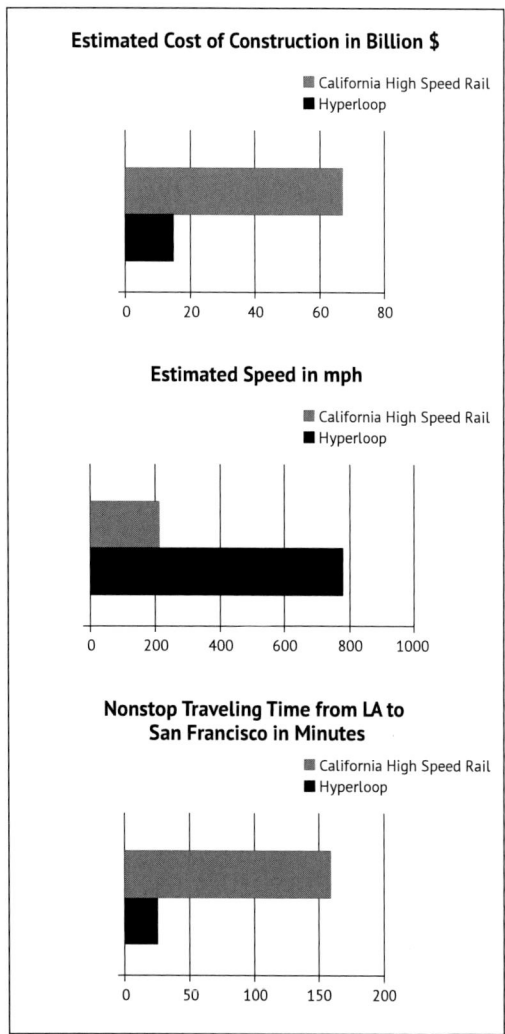

Adapted from Forbes article, "Hyperloop Reality Check:
Elon Musk's High-Speed Scheme Is Alive and Kicking" by Mark
Rogowsky

21

As used in line 13, "question" most nearly means

A) inquiry.
B) doubt.
C) matter.
D) consideration.

22

The central idea of the first paragraph (lines 1-32) is that

A) the author does not approve California's "high speed" rail because of its high cost.
B) a new mode of transportation should be superior to the existing ones in every aspect.
C) the author regards California-based enterprises highly.
D) public transit needs a breakthrough in order to maintain its popularity.

23

Which choice provides the best evidence for the answer to the previous question?

A) Lines 3-8 ("How … world.")
B) Lines 12-16 ("The train … it.")
C) Lines 19-24 ("Compared … transport.")
D) Lines 26-30 ("As things … transit.")

24

Which choice does the author mention as an advantage of supersonic plane?

A) Noiselessness
B) Accessibility
C) Safety
D) Resistance to natural disasters

25

Which choice provides the best evidence for the answer to the previous question?

A) Lines 12-19 ("The train ... massive.")
B) Lines 19-24 ("Compared ... transport.")
C) Lines 33-38 ("The Hyperloop ... cheaper.")
D) Lines 38-42 ("With ... showstopper.")

26

As used in line 37, "suspect" most nearly means

A) doubt.
B) conjecture.
C) conclude.
D) claim.

27

What function does the third paragraph (lines 54-66) serve in the passage as a whole?

A) It provides an alternative to the primary solution suggested in the second paragraph.
B) It describes the pros of a new technology that has been denounced by the author.
C) It illustrates a concept that could potentially solve the issue discussed in the first two paragraphs of the passage.
D) It proposes a solution to the central problem of the passage that will be subsequently argued against.

28

Which choice best supports the conclusion that Hyperloop is only a conceptual transportation system as of now?

A) Teleportation is the only option for high speed travel.
B) Very powerful fans can push air at a high velocity and shoot people-sized pods over long distance.
C) Containing friction created by a massive amount of air traveling at sonic speed inside a tube is virtually impossible.
D) Low pressure containment with devices to prevent air leak can create a very sturdy system.

29

Data in the graphs about Hyperloop and California High Speed Rail most strongly support which of the following statements?

A) Although Hyperloop is very fast, its cost is tremendous.
B) Although Hyperloop boasts a shorter travelling time, California High Speed Rail covers a longer distance.
C) Hyperloop is arguably the best available transportation method for intercity travel.
D) The Hyperloop is over three times faster than California High Speed Rail.

30

Data in the graph provide most direct support for which idea in the passage?

A) Hyperloop is a better transportation method than high speed railway for cities that are less than 900 miles apart.

B) Hyperloop is the best transportation method out there for travelling distances that are sufficiently long.

C) Air travel is inefficient for distances under 900 miles because descending and ascending take up most of the time.

D) Hyperloop has no problem regarding sonic boom, because the super quiet tube will deal with the sound.

31

The graph suggests which of the following about the cost efficiency of the Hyperloop?

A) With extremely low cost, it has medium quality of speed and traveling time.

B) Compared to its cost, it has wonderful speed, but traveling time is substantially extended.

C) The flaw in its traveling time can be compensated with its low cost and high speed.

D) Compared to the California high speed rail, it is more cost-efficient in terms of speed and traveling time.

Questions 32-41 are based on the following passage and supporting material.

The passage is from *The Grand Canyon of Arizona* by William Haskell Simpson, 1920.

Many of those who seek and love earth's greatest scenery have declared that they found it at the Grand Canyon of Arizona. Travelers flock to it from the ends of the earth, though the majority
5 of the visitors, numbering every year about a hundred thousand, are Americans.

The Grand Canyon of the Colorado River, in northern Arizona, is indeed a world wonder, and there is no other chasm in the world worthy to be
10 compared with it. It is more than two hundred miles long, including Marble Canyon, is from ten to thirteen miles wide in the granite gorge section, and is more than a mile deep. It was created ages and ages ago by the erosive action of
15 water, wind, and frost, and it is still being deepened and widened imperceptibly year by year.

The Colorado River, which drains a region of three hundred thousand square miles and is two
20 thousand miles long from the rise of its principal source, is formed in southern Utah by the junction of the Grand and the Green Rivers, and, flowing through Utah and Arizona to tide-water at the Gulf of California, it dashes in, a headless
25 torrent through this titanic gorge—this dream of color, tinted like a rainbow or a sunset.

The canyon is reached by a railroad running to the rim, and may be visited any day in the year. It is unlike most other scenery, because when
30 standing on its rim you look down instead of up. Imagine a gigantic trough, filled with bare mountains on each side and sloping to a narrow channel, which in turn is carved deeply and steeply out of solid granite. You come upon it
35 unawares from the level, timbered, plateau

country. The experience is an absolutely unique one. Only when you go down one of the trails to the bottom and look up is the view more nearly like other grand mountain vistas. The first
40 glimpse always is from the upper edge, and, having no previous standard of measurement, you find it difficult to adjust yourself to this strange condition. The distant rim swims in a bluish haze. The nearer red rocks forming the inner canyon
45 buttes—crowned with massive table—lands that look like temples, minarets, and battlements— reflect the sunlight in myriad hues. It seems a vast illusion rather than reality. No wonder that the first look often awes the spectator into silence
50 and tears!

But, before you have been here long, you will wish to know how it all happened. You will ask how the canyon was made.

Just between ourselves, no one absolutely can
55 tell just how the miracle occurred, for no human being was there at the time. But the geologist has put together, bit by bit, thousands of facts, dug from the rocks which here lie exposed like a mammoth layer-cake and his explanation is so
60 convincing that it must stand as at least the probable truth.

Here may be seen rocks of the four geological periods which are among the very oldest of our earth. The rocks of later periods were here once,
65 too, making a layer more than two miles high resting on what is to-day the top, but in some remote age they were shaved off by some great natural force, perhaps a glacier.

The eating away of the rocks which formed
70 the canyon itself is modern. Scientists say it was done, as it were, last Monday or Tuesday, for it was when the top two thirds had been "shaved off," as we have said, that the Colorado River began to cut the Grand Canyon through the rocks
75 that formed the lower third.

While the cracking of the crust, caused by internal fires, may have helped the process of canyon-making, the result of erosion is seen everywhere. Every passing shower, every desert
80 wind, every snowfall, changes the contour of the region imperceptibly but surely. The canyon is Nature's open book in which we may read how the earth was built.

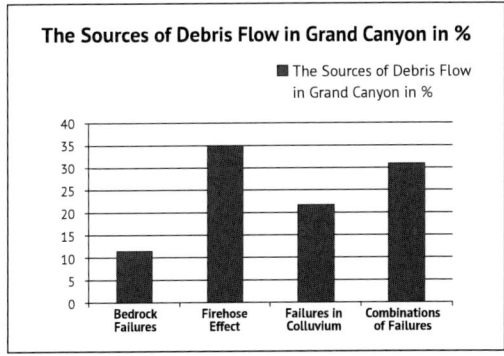

(Source: U.S. Geological Survey, Initiation and Frequency of Debris Flows in Grand Canyon, Arizona, modified from Melis and others, 1994)

32

According to the passage, the depth and width of the Grand Canyon are

A) equal to those of some of the greatest canyons around the world.
B) the result of the Colorado River's erosion an extremely long time ago.
C) even more impressive when viewed from the bottom.
D) increasing very slightly each year.

33

Which choice provides the best evidence for the answer to the previous question?

A) Lines 3-6 ("Travelers ... Americans.")
B) Lines 10-13 ("It ... deep.")
C) Lines 13-17 ("It ... year.")
D) Lines 18-21 ("The ... source.")

34

As used in line 24, "dashes" most nearly means

A) rushes.
B) hurls.
C) shatters.
D) destroys.

35

The fourth paragraph (lines 27-50) primarily serves to

A) explain the geographic composition of a landmark.
B) contrast two different perspectives of a natural phenomenon.
C) address the historical importance of a tourist attraction.
D) descriptively extol the beauty of a unique landscape.

36

In the passage, it is implied that the origin of the Grand Canyon

A) is a point of universal curiosity for the many tourists, especially Americans, who visit it annually.
B) is influenced by erosion but is principally due to the cracking of the crust by internal fires.
C) is seen by the transition of rock type from the uppermost layer to the bottom one.
D) cannot be definitely ascertained, but can be accurately conjectured through careful study.

37

Which choice provides the best evidence for the answer to the previous question?

A) Lines 13-15 ("It ... frost.")
B) Lines 51-53 ("But ... made.")
C) Lines 54-61 ("Just ... truth.")
D) Lines 62-64 ("Here ... earth.")

38

As used in line 60, "stand" most nearly means

A) rise.
B) reject.
C) remain valid.
D) shine.

39

Data in the graph about the sources of debris flow in Grand Canyon most strongly support which of the following statements?

A) Out of a variety of causes, "Combinations of Failures" is the single most important factor.
B) "Combinations of Failures" is most likely to cause debris flow, because it is responsible for a high percentage of debris flow despite the fact that it rarely occurs.
C) The "Firehose Effect" is the single greatest contributor to debris flow in the Grand Canyon, despite the fact that it is the rarest of all causes of debris flow.
D) "Bedrock Failures" is seldom responsible for debris flow.

40

Data in the graph indicate that

A) debris flow in the Grand Canyon is strong enough to cause various failures.
B) the failures in the graph do not comprise the complete list of causes of debris flow.
C) "Combination of Failures" leads to more debris flow than does the "Firehose Effect."
D) none of the failures causes over half of the debris flow in the Grand Canyon.

41

According to the graph, the "Firehose Effect" is shown as

A) the most important source of debris flow in the Grand Canyon.
B) the least important source of debris flow in the Grand Canyon.
C) the source of all debris flow in the Grand Canyon.
D) one of the biggest problems the residents of the Grand Canyon face.

Question 42-52 are based on the following passage.

Passage 1 is an excerpt from *To the Person Sitting in Darkness* by Mark Twain in an article addressed to the Anti-Imperialist League of New York, 1901. Written in response to increasing violence on the part of imperial and colonial powers, Twain speaks to "Our Brother who Sits in Darkness", an ironic name for indigenous people affected by colonialism. Passage 2 is an excerpt from *The Strenuous Life*, a speech given in 1899 by Theodore Roosevelt.

Passage 1

Extending the Blessings of Civilization to our Brother who Sits in Darkness has been a good trade and has paid well, on the whole; and there
Line is money in it yet, if carefully worked—but not
5 enough, in my judgement, to make any considerable risk advisable. The People that Sit in Darkness are getting to be too scarce—too scarce and too shy. And such darkness as is now left is really of but an indifferent quality, and not dark
10 enough for the game. Most of those People that Sit in Darkness have been furnished with more light than was good for them or profitable for us. We have been injudicious. We have forgotten our primary goal: to "face the responsibilities with
15 proper seriousness, courage, and high resolve".

The Blessings-of-Civilization Trust, wisely and cautiously administered, is a Daisy. There is more money in it, more territory, more sovereignty, and other kinds of emolument, than
20 there is in any other game that is played. But Christendom has been playing it badly of late years, and must certainly suffer by it, in my opinion. She has been so eager to get every stake that appeared on the green cloth, that the People
25 who Sit in Darkness have noticed it—they have noticed it, and have begun to show alarm. They have become suspicious of the Blessings of Civilization. More—they have begun to examine

them. This is not well. The Blessings of
Civilization are all right, and a good commercial
property; there could not be a better, in a dim
light. In the right kind of a light, and at a proper
distance, with the goods a little out of focus, they
furnish this desirable exhibit to the Gentlemen
who Sit in Darkness:

*Love, Justice, Gentleness, Christianity, Protection
to the Weak, Temperance, Law and Order, Liberty,
Equality, Honorable Dealing, Mercy, Education*
—and so on.

There. Is it good? Sir, it is pie. It will bring into camp any idiot that sits in darkness anywhere. But not if we adulterate it. It is proper to be emphatic upon that point. This brand is strictly for Export—apparently. Apparently. Privately and confidentially, it is nothing of the kind. Privately and confidentially, it is merely an outside cover, gay and pretty and attractive, displaying the special patterns of our Civilization which we reserve for Home Consumption, while inside the bale is the Actual Thing that the Customer Sitting in Darkness buys with his blood and tears and land and liberty. That Actual Thing is, indeed, Civilization, but it is only for Export. Is there a difference between the two brands? In some of the details, yes.

We all know that the Business is being ruined. The reason is not far to seek. It is because our Mr. McKinley, and Mr. Chamberlain, and the Kaiser, and the Czar and the French have been exporting the Actual Thing with the outside cover left off. This is bad for the Game. It shows that these new players of it are not sufficiently acquainted with it.

Passage 2

We cannot sit huddled within our own borders and avow ourselves merely an assemblage of well-to-do hucksters who care nothing for what happens beyond. Such a policy would defeat even its own end; for as the nations grow to have ever wider and wider interests, and are brought into closer and closer contact, if we are to hold our own in the struggle for naval and commercial supremacy, we must build up our power without our own borders. We must build the isthmian canal, and we must grasp the points of vantage which will enable us to have our say in deciding the destiny of the oceans of the East and the West.

So much for the commercial side. From the standpoint of international honor the argument is even stronger. The guns that thundered off Manila and Santiago left us echoes of glory, but they also left us a legacy of duty. If we drove out a medieval tyranny only to make room for savage anarchy, we had better not have begun the task at all. It is worse than idle to say that we have no duty to perform, and can leave to their fates the islands we have conquered. Such a course would be the course of infamy. It would be followed at once by utter chaos in the wretched islands themselves. Some stronger, manlier power would have to step in and do the work, and we would have shown ourselves weaklings, unable to carry to successful completion the labors that great and high-spirited nations are eager to undertake.

The work must be done; we cannot escape our responsibility; and if we are worth our salt, we shall be glad of the chance to do the work—glad of the chance to show ourselves equal to one of the great tasks set modern civilization. But let us not deceive ourselves as to the importance of the task. Let us not be misled by vain glory into underestimating the strain it will put on our powers. Above all, let us, as we value our own self-

respect, face the responsibilities with proper
105 seriousness, courage, and high resolve. We must demand the highest order of integrity and ability in our public men who are to grapple with these new problems. We must hold to a rigid accountability those public servants who show
110 unfaithfulness to the interests of the nation or inability to rise to the high level of the new demands upon our strength and our resources.

42

It can be inferred that the author of Passage 1 believes that imperialistic policies

A) benefit both the colonies and the mother country through commerce.
B) focus on exporting goods to less developed countries and boost their economies.
C) intrude upon the native population's life in an undesirable way.
D) have successfully civilized and evangelized the indigenous people.

43

Which choices provides the best evidence for the answer to the previous question?

A) Lines 1-6 ("Extending … advisable")
B) Lines 23-29 ("She has … them")
C) Lines 29-32 ("The Blessings … light")
D) Lines 40-44 ("It will … apparently")

44

As used in line 11, "furnished" most nearly means

A) illuminated.
B) provided.
C) armed.
D) decorated.

45

According to the first paragraph (lines 64-77) of Passage 2, in order for the nation to guard its supremacy over others, it must

A) extend its power and influence overseas.
B) constantly compete with other nations militarily.
C) isolate itself and settle its domestic issues.
D) seize absolute power of its colonies.

46

As used in line 107, "grapple with" most nearly means

A) deal with.
B) seize.
C) fight with.
D) grasp.

47

In Passage 2, the speaker argues that countries without a leader can

A) rebuild themselves both politically and economically.
B) be thrown into political turmoil.
C) easily be seized by a tyrannical dictator.
D) be annexed by other powerful countries.

48

Which choice provides the best evidence for the answer to the previous question?

A) Lines 82-87 ("If we … conquered.")
B) Lines 90-94 ("Some … undertake.")
C) Lines 95-99 ("The work … civilization.")
D) Lines 101-105 ("Let us … resolve.")

49

In lines 14-15, the author of Passage 1 refers to a statement made in Passage 2 in order to

A) question the claim made in Passage 2 that imperialism is necessary for a nation to prosper.
B) agree with the opinion about expansionism discussed in the first sentence of Passage 2.
C) point out that the nation has failed to live up to its initial intentions regarding overseas intervention given in Passage 2.
D) strengthen the reasoning behind the nation's decision to support small countries made in Passage 2.

50

Which choice best represents the relationship between Passage 1 and Passage 2?

A) Passage 2 restates the same idea in Passage 1 but in a different tone.
B) Passage 2 provides a more detailed explanation of the claim made in Passage 1.
C) Passage 2 presents a different view on an issue discussed in Passage 1.
D) Passage 2 supports the point of view in Passage 1 with further evidence.

51

The authors of both passages would most likely agree with which of the following statements about the United States in the late-19th and early-20th century?

A) The nation treated the Native Americans very poorly.
B) Americans were strongly inclined towards anti-expansion sentiments.
C) Americans fully advocated the nation's foreign policies.
D) The nation was well aware of the possibility of increasing its international influence.

52

How would the author of Passage 1 respond to the claims made in the final paragraph of Passage 2?

A) The United States has failed to carry out its duties properly and faithfully as intended.
B) Imperialism's fundamental concern should be the welfare of the colonies.
C) Expansionism can never benefit the colonies' native populations in any way.
D) The nation should strive to conquer more countries in order to achieve world peace.

STOP
If you finish before time is called, you may check your work on this section only.
Do not turn to any other section.

No Test Material On This Page

Writing and Language Test

35 MINUTES, 44 QUESTIONS

Turn to Section 2 of your answer sheet to answer the questions in this section.

DIRECTIONS

Each passage below is accompanied by a number of questions. For some questions, you will consider how the passage might be revised to improve the expression of ideas. For other questions, you will consider how the passage might be edited to correct errors in sentence structure, usage, or punctuation. A passage or a question may be accompanied by one or more graphics (such as a table or graph) that you will consider as you make revising and editing decisions.

Some questions will direct you to an underlined portion of a passage. Other questions will direct you to a location in a passage or ask you to think about the passage as a whole.

After reading each passage, choose the answer to each question that most effectively improves the quality of writing in the passage or that makes the passage conform to the conventions of standard written English. Many questions include a "NO CHANGE" option. Choose that option if you think the best choice is to leave the relevant portion of the passage as it is.

Questions 1-11 are based on the following passage.

One Too Many Prisoners

A major concern throughout our state is incarceration rates, **1** it is rising every year. Our prisons are at full capacity. It looks as though we should either build new holding facilities or resort to other measures, such as early parole. The biggest obstacle, **2** however, is that there are problems to every course of action that has been proposed. Lowered property values often result from prisons.

1
A) NO CHANGE
B) every year they are rising
C) which are rising every year
D) every year rising

2
A) NO CHANGE
B) however
C) neverthless,
D) therefore,

In the case of early release of prisoners, you get [3] fears, of increased crime rates. Local populations are criticized for not wanting to live near a correctional facility, but honestly, who would?

[4] Most of the opposition is not unreasonable since the solutions are closely tied to local economy. Community outreach programs, though expensive, can achieve great success, but citizens protest that increased government spending leads to higher taxes. Some industries benefit from the inexpensive labor that prison populations [5] disseminate and generally reject calls to reduce incarceration rates.

Maybe those of us who are worried should look into other methods that communities can use to [6] lower the numbers of people being put in prison.

3

A) NO CHANGE
B) fears:
C) fears
D) fears—

4

Which choice best connects this paragraph with the previous paragraph?
A) NO CHANGE
B) What makes the problem even trickier is that
C) A related and interesting fact is that
D) Some social scientists argue that

5

A) NO CHANGE
B) bestow
C) grant
D) provide

6

A) NO CHANGE
B) lowers
C) lowering
D) lowered

According to a study, 49% of offenders who have not committed severe crimes such as sexual assault or murder, were raised either in a family with an annual income lower than $5,000 or under abusive parents or guardians. [7] They prove that the environment in which a person grows can significantly influence his or her vulnerability to committing crimes.

[8] Therefore, we need to ensure a healthy growing environment for children and teenagers. We can provide them the financial and emotional support they need. By doing so, juvenile crime rate will drop in half, the overall crime rate by 23%, and the incarceration rate [9] drops by 18%.

7
A) NO CHANGE
B) These statistics
C) Those
D) We

8
Which choice most effectively combines the underlined sentences?
A) By providing them the financial and emotional support they need, therefore, we need to ensure a healthy growing environment for children and teenagers.
B) Therefore we need, by providing a financial and emotional support they need, to ensure a healthy growing environment for children and teenagers.
C) Therefore, we need to ensure a healthy and growing environment for children and teenagers by providing them the financial and emotional support they need.
D) A healthy growing environment for children and teenagers needs to be ensured, therefore; we can provide them the financial and emotional support they need.

9
A) NO CHANGE
B) will drop by
C) by
D) DELETE the underlined portion.

Furthermore, we should support programs that pay special attention to already released convicts [10] to prevent them from taking paths that will return them to institutions. More than half of released convicts are re-incarcerated within a month of release, which only serves to worsen incarceration rates.

[11] Surely we should make certain that individual citizens, organizations, and all levels of society work together to solve the problem of high incarceration rates while we still have a chance to save a generation of young and disadvantaged people.

10

Which choice most effectively sets up the information that follows?
A) NO CHANGE
B) and help them find a better job than they had before.
C) through programs that prepare them to return to society.
D) who are probably very likely to commit the same crime.

11

At this point, the writer is considering adding the following sentence.

Through these programs, combined with raised awareness for the negative effects of having too many people in prison, we can help the future generation.

Should the writer make this addition here?
A) Yes, because it introduces a concern for the future generation in the passage, which is repeated in the following sentence.
B) Yes, because it summarizes the arguments that have been made so far about programs discussed in the passage.
C) No, because it brings up an irrelevant point about the number of prisoners, which is not mentioned again.
D) No, because it contradicts the claim made earlier in the passage about the uselessness of government programs due to the high cost.

Questions 12-22 are based on the following passage.

A Symphony of Pain: Majoring in Music

By the end of the year, I had given up classical music for good. I'd had enough of glissando thumbs, enough of pounding on black-and-white keys for ten hours straight in a cramped room every day. I'd had enough of **12** reiterating the same song repetitively in my head until it became stripped of all emotion and became a clatter of meaningless noise. I had endured enough of wooden switches **13** being cracked my fingers and shoulders, sometimes my face. I was improving my technical skill **14** at the price of all my enjoyment in it. **15** Additionally, when college applications rolled around, I horrified my teachers, my parents, and my musical friends by ditching music to pursue a major in ecology.

12
A) NO CHANGE
B) repeating the same melody
C) duplicating the same piece over and over again
D) repetitively replaying the same tune

13
A) NO CHANGE
B) having cracked
C) cracking
D) cracked

14
Which of the following results in a sentence that best supports the main point of this paragraph?
A) NO CHANGE
B) but my health was rapidly failing.
C) to the point where I had mixed up my priorities.
D) until it came before true success.

15
A) NO CHANGE
B) Nevertheless,
C) Likewise,
D) Consequently,

"*Ecology?*" my parents shouted. "Is that what you're going to do, use fingers that played Stravinsky to pick up trash?" To them, over ten years of expensive lessons and enforced practice had ended in a failure of a daughter. [16] My parents' disappointment was the least of my [17] problems, however, I was already falling into depression from the abuse and stress I had endured for years.

[1]Despite being used as an excuse for torture, music was (and is) an object of devout admiration. [2] In a 2003 poll, it was shown that over 70% of Americans believed learning music helped in learning other subjects and in preventing disciplinary problems, while 95% believed that it was an essential part of a well-rounded education.

16

At this point, the writer wishes to add this sentence:

Over 60% of parents are known to protest when their children change majors.

Should the writer add this sentence here?

A) Yes, because it supports the behavior demonstrated in the preceding sentence.
B) Yes, because it supplies quantitative information about an abstract principle described in the paragraph.
C) No, because it takes the focus of the paragraph away from the main point to a loosely related detail.
D) No, because it simply repeats the claim made in the previous sentence.

17

A) NO CHANGE
B) problems—however, I
C) problems. However, I
D) problems, however. I

[3] Numerous theories about the spatial-temporal benefits of piano lessons and the boost that it could give underachievers have been presented. [4] Unfortunately, this reverence for music is badly marred by the way we approach the subject. [18]

Anyone planning to major in music must be [19] <u>tough-skinned survivors and stoics</u>. Although ostensibly used to push students to their full potential, [20] <u>music classes</u> will leave them deeply shaken. The movie *Whiplash* shows the worst of musical [21] <u>tyranny: bleeding hands, hurled chairs, trembling shoulders, maniac professors,</u> and highlights the abuse that is inflicted in a destructive teacher-student relationship. The movie certainly exaggerated some of the violence for dramatic purposes, but the reality is almost as frightening.

18

To make this paragraph most logical, sentence 2 should be
A) placed where it is now.
B) placed before sentence 1.
C) placed after sentence 4.
D) DELETED from the paragraph.

19

A) NO CHANGE
B) tough-skinned, both as survivors and stoics.
C) both tough-skinned survivors and stoics.
D) a tough-skinned, stoical survivor.

20

A) NO CHANGE
B) the decision to major in music
C) the harsh methods used in music classes
D) they should be wary of majoring in music because it

21

A) NO CHANGE
B) tyranny—bleeding hands, hurled chairs, trembling shoulders, maniac professors—
C) tyranny, bleeding hands, hurled chairs, trembling shoulders, maniac professors,
D) tyranny; bleeding hands, hurled chairs, trembling shoulders, maniac professors;

[22] Prominent music professors have been known to rip their students' music sheets in half and fling it in their face. My mother, who used to be a pianist, particularly remembers one professor who could not tolerate any of her mistakes. Once, when she made a mistake during an important recital, her professor walked up to her and hissed with quiet fury, "If you keep playing like this, you will never learn from me again." My mother, crying, went home and practiced until she could play the whole song blindfolded.

22
A) NO CHANGE
B) Prioritized
C) Empathetic
D) Emulated

Questions 23-33 are based on the following passage.

Mind-blowing Consequences of Wind

Wind has literally shaped our planet for thousands of years— **23** eroding, deflating, cooling, and dispersing. It sculpts mountains, moves dust across continents thousands of kilometers apart, and stirs oceans to make nutrient-rich currents flow and waves churn stormily. **24** Thus, it plants seeds, spores, and pollen in different locations, picking up the potential for new life and helping it bear fruit.

The wind can cause the smallest bits of dust to fly to another part of the **25** world; where they strike against larger objects when they land. The wind serves as heaven's invisible arms, and the dust gather together to form a hammer. Using the smallest fragments of our planet, the wind molds the geography of the Earth, from mushrooming rock formations **26** and honey-gold sanddunes.

23
A) NO CHANGE
B) it has eroded, deflated, cooled, and dispersed.
C) while erosion, deflation, cooling, and dispersion have been used.
D) and eroding, deflating, cooling, and dispersing.

24
A) NO CHANGE
B) Nevertheless,
C) Hence,
D) Moreover,

25
A) NO CHANGE
B) world, where
C) world—where
D) world, where,

26
A) NO CHANGE
B) or
C) to
D) including

The wind not only shapes our soil, but the life that grows within it. Seeds also use the wind for transportation, floating gently on the currents of air or falling to the ground. **27** [1] While the wind gives birth and spreads plant life, it also serves to prune it. [2] High winds can tear up trees, snap off thinner branches, and keep plants in control. [3] Animals also depend on the wind for survival. [4] Birds jump onto the wind to carry them long distances, while cockroaches sense the tingle of wind that **28** comes before predator attacks to flee. **29** [5] Elk sniff the wind to **30** find out if predators are coming, while glaucous gulls feel the wind to know the right timing to attack.

27

At this point, the writer is considering adding the following information.

Pollen can also hitch a ride, especially when similar plants are grouped together.

Should the writer make this addition here?

A) Yes, because it supports the claim that plants depend on wind.
B) Yes, because it demonstrates the key role of concentration of plants in wind dissemination.
C) No, because it contradicts the previous statement about wind being used for transportation.
D) No, because it shifts the focus of the paragraph from transportation to dissemination.

28

A) NO CHANGE
B) blows when predators attack, so they can flee.
C) warns them to flee from predators.
D) they flee from before predators attack.

29

Where is the most logical place in the passage to add the following sentence?

However, wind is not always beneficial.

A) Before sentence 1
B) After sentence 1
C) After sentence 2
D) After sentence 3

30

A) NO CHANGE
B) know why
C) smell out the
D) wonder if

When wind grows cold, it can pierce through the thick wool of sheep and cause them to fall sick. It also attacks penguins: although their fat and feathers keep them warm, their flippers and [31] feet are vulnerable to cold winds. Flying insects get caught up in winds and killed. But the damage of wind has been greatly exacerbated by human mistakes.

31
A) NO CHANGE
B) feet are taken
C) feet become attached
D) feet freeze

In the past, even as the wind uprooted them, trees with thick trunks and strong branches would restrain the wind from getting carried away by its own strength. Their firm roots would anchor the fertile dirt (called loess) in which plant life could thrive, preventing the loess from being swept away by the wind. However, deforestation has affected the wind as well. [32] Loess is thinned as the number of trees decreases. Desert winds have grown stronger with nothing to stop them, [33] the sky reddens and rain is blocked. Drought and dust outbreaks have grown, while the worsening air quality has led to the decline of coral reefs. Sand and topsoil tearing apart the cells of delicate plants, exposing them to the worst effects of evaporation and drought.

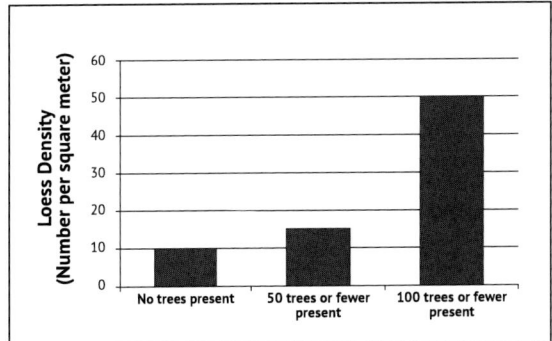

Effect of the Presence of Trees on Loess Density

Adapted from Vern Hofman and Dave Franzen (1997). "Emergency Tillage to Control Wind Erosion".
North Dakota State University Extension Service.

32

Which choice offers an accurate interpretation of the data in the chart?
A) The bar graphs are lower in Loess density with fewer trees present.
B) Loess is reduced as wind velocity increases.
C) Loess density decreases proportionally as the number of trees decreases.
D) Just fifty trees are enough to double the amount of loess retained.

33

A) NO CHANGE
B) reddening the sky and blocking rain.
C) making the sky red and the rain blocked.
D) —the sky reddens, rain stops.

Questions 34-44 are based on the following passage.

Adapting to The New Media

Many fans consider film adaptations of [34] his or her favorite novels and comic books disappointing and disrespectful at best. Attempts at filming the *Twilight* series caused angry blacklash from purists, those who expect Hollywood to follow the original source material page by page. [35] The only positive reviews claimed that they were happy that there were no more books left for the studios to mangle. Isn't the author dismayed to see her work disfigured so horribly for moviegoing audiences? Another supposed outrage is *The Great Gatsby 3D*, an adaptation of F. Scott Fitzgerald's 1925 novel. Imagine taking a novel about capitalist excess and filming it [36] in a capitalistically excessive way.

34
A) NO CHANGE
B) one's
C) their
D) oneself's

35
At this point, the writer wishes to add the following statement.

Purists are sometimes seen as radical because they do not allow any room for personal interpretations.

Should the writer add this sentence here?
A) Yes, because it offers additional information about purists.
B) Yes, because it supports the main idea of this paragraph about opposing film adaptations.
C) No, because it discusses information that has never been introduced in the paragraph.
D) No, because it provides information that is irrelevant to the passage.

36
A) NO CHANGE
B) with capitalist excess
C) in a way that is capitalistically excessive
D) excessively capitalistic.

I see nothing wrong with creative interpretations. I do not see them as [37] damaged the novel. [38] After all, didn't *Twilight*'s creator borrow heavily from other writers' ideas? For example, the notion of vampires is a myth stretching back centuries. And as for her work [39] disfiguring, I'm sure the millions of dollars she made in rights can ease her pain. No doubt she recognizes her characters in the movie as slightly altered versions of her original concepts. Fitzgerald, too, would see support for his criticisms of the American dream in the ironic, over-the-top nature of the most recent film.

[40] I believe that Hollywood has done a fairly decent job, at least not as terrible as the criticizers claim. Sometimes, the filmmaker needs to show a character's whole lifetime in two [41] hours. The process is not an easy task.

37
A) NO CHANGE
B) having damaged
C) damaging
D) damage

38
A) NO CHANGE
B) In contrast,
C) Likewise,
D) Nonetheless,

39
A) NO CHANGE
B) disfigures,
C) having disfigured,
D) being disfigured,

40
Which choice most effectively introduces the information that follows?
A) *The Shawshank Redemption*, adapted from Stephen King's novella was applauded by many critics.
B) It may be the actors' performance that bothers the audience.
C) Limitation certainly exists in reproducing the whole book on screen.
D) Film adaptations have shown great improvements recently.

41
Which choice most logically combines the sentences at the underlined portion?
A) hours, which is not
B) hours and that is not
C) hours, not being
D) hours, not

[42] Because *Twilight* fans complain about the movie ruining the novel, the novel has raised about $400 million worldwide and conduced the audience to buy the book in order to have a more exact and detailed knowledge about the story and characters. Isn't that the whole point of film adaptations? To outshine the book?

The fact that literature is about interpretations [43] so makes *The Great Gatsby 3D* an excellent film adaptation. Baz Luhrmann, the film director, [44] successfully interprets the novel in his own way and by doing so, has left room for the audience for their personal opinions about the novel. Fans might not welcome the diverse adaptations, but I believe that they have actually helped enrich the novels.

42
A) NO CHANGE
B) Although
C) While
D) Since

43
A) NO CHANGE
B) and
C) which
D) DELETE the underlined portion

44
A) NO CHANGE
B) having successfully interpreted
C) successfully interpreting
D) has successfully interpreted

STOP

If you finish before time is called, you may check your work on this section only.
Do not turn to any other section.

No Test Material On This Page

3

Math Test (No Calculator)
25 MINUTES, 20 QUESTIONS

Turn to Section 3 of your answer sheet to answer the questions in this section.

DIRECTIONS

For questions 1-15, solve each problem, choose the best answer from the choices provided, and fill in the corresponding circle on your answer sheet. **For questions 16-20,** solve the problem and enter your answer in the grid on the answer sheet. Please refer to the directions before question 16 on how to enter your answers in the grid. You may use any available space in your test booklet for scratch work.

NOTES

1. The use of a calculator **is not permitted.**
2. All variables and expressions used represent real numbers unless otherwise indicated.
3. Figures provided in this test are drawn to scale unless otherwise indicated.
4. All figures lie in a plane unless otherwise indicated.
5. Unless otherwise indicated, the domain of a given function f is the set of all real numbers x for which $f(x)$ is a real number.

REFERENCE

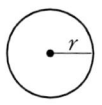 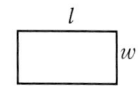 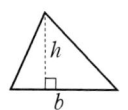 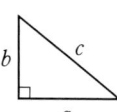 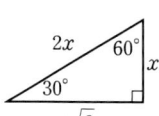 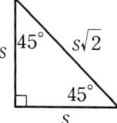

$A=\pi r^2$ $A=lw$ $A=\frac{1}{2}bh$ $c^2=a^2+b^2$ Special Right Triangles
$C=2\pi r$

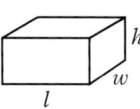 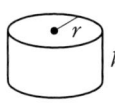 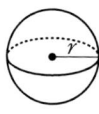 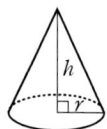 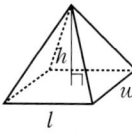

$V=lwh$ $V=\pi r^2 h$ $V=\frac{4}{3}\pi r^3$ $V=\frac{1}{3}\pi r^2 h$ $V=\frac{1}{3}lwh$

The number of degrees of arc in a circle is 360.
The number of radians of arc in a circle is 2π.
The sum of the measures in degrees of the angles of a triangle is 180.

3

1

If $\dfrac{y+3}{y-4}=12$, what is the value of y?

A) $-\dfrac{51}{13}$

B) 6

C) $\dfrac{45}{11}$

D) $\dfrac{51}{11}$

2

If $f(x)=\dfrac{x}{3}-7$, what is the value of $f(-6)$?

A) -13

B) -9

C) -5

D) 13

3

$$x-y=2$$
$$2x+3y=39$$

Which of the following ordered pairs $(x,\ y)$ satisfies the system of equations above?

A) $(7,\ 9)$

B) $(9,\ 7)$

C) $(13,\ 11)$

D) $(11,\ 13)$

4

If $\dfrac{c+2d}{c}=\dfrac{7}{16}$, which of the following must also be true?

A) $\dfrac{d}{c}=\dfrac{32}{9}$

B) $c=\dfrac{9}{32}d$

C) $d=\dfrac{9}{32}c$

D) $\dfrac{c}{d}=-\dfrac{32}{9}$

5

If the expression below were simplified to the form ax^2+bx+c, where a, b, and c are constants, what is the value of a^2-b?

$$5(x^2-2x+3)-3(2x^2-x+4)$$

A) 2

B) 6

C) 8

D) 14

6

For the function $f(x)=-2x^2+5x-c$, where c is a constant, if $f(0)=2$, what is the value of $f(1)$?

A) 1

B) 2

C) 5

D) 6

7

In preparation for a taekwondo competition, Harper devised a training regime in which the number of wooden planks she chopped increased every week starting from the second week, by a constant amount. Harper's training regime is such that the number of wooden planks she chopped in week 2 was 4 and the number of wooden planks she chopped in week 12 was 9. Based on this relationship and information, which of the following best describes how the number of chopped planks changes between week 2 and week 12 of her training regime?

A) Harper chops through 1 more plank of wood every week.

B) Harper chops through 5 more planks of wood every week.

C) Harper chops through half a plank of wood more every 2 weeks.

D) Harper chops through 1 more plank of wood every 2 weeks.

8

Which of the following equations has a graph in the xy-plane for which y is always greater than or equal to -2?

A) $y = x^2 - 3$

B) $y = (x-2)^3$

C) $y = x - 2$

D) $y = |x| - 2$

9

Which of the following is equivalent to the expression below?

$$4a^4 - 12a^2b^3 + 9b^6$$

A) $(2a^2 - 3b^3)^2$

B) $(2a^2 + 3b^3)^2$

C) $(2a - 3b^2)^2$

D) $(2a^4 - 3b^2)^2$

10

If $\dfrac{k+3}{k-3} = 18$, what is the value of k?

A) 3

B) 17

C) 18

D) $\dfrac{57}{17}$

11

$$y = 3x - 1$$
$$2xy = -x + 1$$

If $x > 0$ in the system of equations above, what is the value of $x - y$?

A) 2

B) 1

C) 0

D) -1

12

A toy store charges $12 for each fire truck and $17 for each train. A mother buys t fire trucks and $2f$ trains for her son. Which of the following represents how much she spends in total?

A) $34f + 12t$

B) $24f + 34t$

C) $12f + 34t$

D) $12f + 17t$

14

In the quadratic equation below, p and q are constants. What are the solutions of the equation when solved for x?

$$2x^2 = p + \frac{q}{4}x$$

A) $x = \dfrac{q}{16} \pm \dfrac{\sqrt{\dfrac{q^2}{16} + 8p}}{4}$

B) $x = \dfrac{q}{4} \pm \sqrt{\dfrac{\dfrac{q^2}{16} + 4p}{4}}$

C) $x = \dfrac{q}{4} \pm \sqrt{\dfrac{\dfrac{q^2}{16} - 8p}{4}}$

D) $x = \dfrac{q}{16} \pm \dfrac{\sqrt{\dfrac{q^2}{4} + 4p}}{4}$

13

$$\frac{5i - 15}{2 + i}$$

If the expression above is rewritten in the form of $a + bi$, where a and b are real numbers, what is the value of $a + b$? ($i = \sqrt{-1}$)

A) -10

B) 0

C) 5

D) 10

15

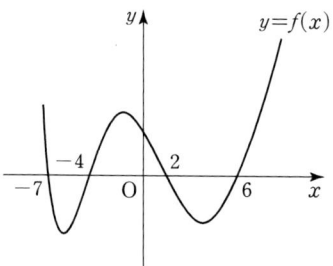

The function $y = f(x)$ is graphed as above. Which of the following could define $f(x)$?

A) $f(x) = (x-2)(x-6)(x+4)(x+7)$

B) $f(x) = (x+2)(x-6)(x-4)(x+7)$

C) $f(x) = (x+2)(x+6)(x-4)(x-7)$

D) $f(x) = (x-2)(x+6)(x+4)(x-7)$

3

DIRECTIONS

For questions 16-20, solve the problem and enter your answer in the grid, as described below, on the answer sheet.

1. Although not required, it is suggested that you write your answer in the boxes at the top of the columns to help you fill in the circles accurately. You will receive credit only if the circles are filled in correctly.

2. Mark no more than one circle in any column.

3. No question has a negative answer.

4. Some problems may have more than one correct answer. In such cases, grid only one answer.

5. **Mixed numbers** such as $3\frac{1}{2}$ must be gridded as 3.5 or 7/2. (If [3 1/2] is entered into the grid, it will be interpreted as $\frac{31}{2}$, not $3\frac{1}{2}$.)

6. **Decimal answers**: If you obtain a decimal answer with more digits than the grid can accommodate, it may be either rounded or truncated, but it must fill the entire grid.

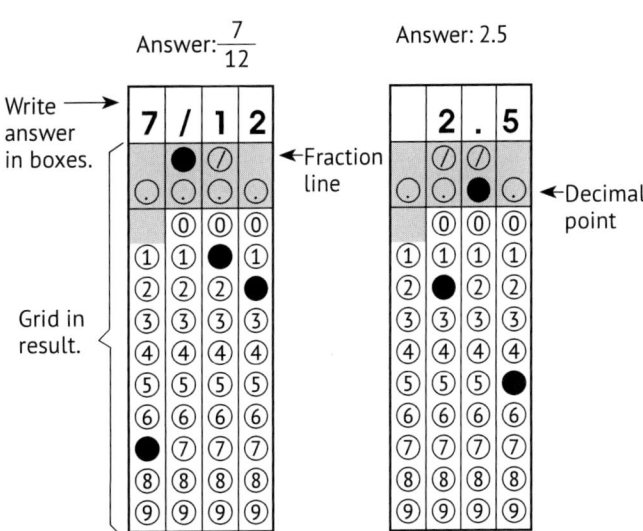

Answer: $\frac{7}{12}$

Answer: 2.5

Acceptable ways to grid $\frac{2}{3}$ are:

Answer: 201 - either position is correct.

NOTE: You may start your answer in any column, space permitting. Columns you don't need to use should be left blank.

CONTINUE

16

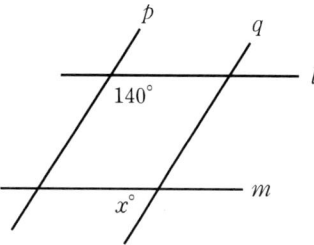

In the figure above, lines ℓ and m are parallel and lines p and q are parallel. What is the value of x? Disregard the degree sign when gridding in your answer.

17

In a right triangle, one angle measures $a°$, where $\sin a° = \frac{5}{13}$. What is $\cos(90° - a°)$?

18

The equation $\dfrac{12x^2 + 4x - 5}{2x - 3k} = 6x + 11 + \dfrac{28}{2x - 3k}$ is true for all values of $x \neq \frac{3}{2}k$, where k is a constant. What is the value of k?

19

$$\frac{x}{3} - y = \frac{4}{9}$$

$$3x + \frac{1}{2}y = 6$$

If (x, y) is the solution of the systems of equations above, what is the value of y?

20

Lee has written 50 words in his book so far. After 20 minutes, his book would contain 410 words. Assuming he writes at the same rate without taking any breaks, how many words will his manuscript contain after an hour and a half?

STOP

If you finish before time is called, you may check your work on this section only.
Do not turn to any other section.

4

Math Test (Calculator)
55 MINUTES, 38 QUESTIONS

Turn to Section 4 of your answer sheet to answer the questions in this section.

DIRECTIONS

For questions 1-30, solve each problem, choose the best answer from the choices provided, and fill in the corresponding circle on your answer sheet. **For questions 31-38,** solve the problem and enter your answer in the grid on the answer sheet. Please refer to the directions before question 31 on how to enter your answers in the grid. You may use any available space in your test booklet for scratch work.

NOTES

1. The use of a calculator **is permitted**.
2. All variables and expressions used represent real numbers unless otherwise indicated.
3. Figures provided in this test are drawn to scale unless otherwise indicated.
4. All figures lie in a plane unless otherwise indicated.
5. Unless otherwise indicated, the domain of a given function f is the set of all real numbers x for which $f(x)$ is a real number.

REFERENCE

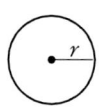

$A = \pi r^2$
$C = 2\pi r$

$A = lw$

$A = \frac{1}{2}bh$

$c^2 = a^2 + b^2$

Special Right Triangles

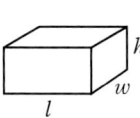

$V = lwh$

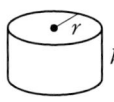

$V = \pi r^2 h$

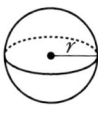

$V = \frac{4}{3}\pi r^3$

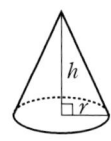

$V = \frac{1}{3}\pi r^2 h$

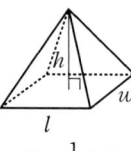

$V = \frac{1}{3}lwh$

The number of degrees of arc in a circle is 360.
The number of radians of arc in a circle is 2π.
The sum of the measures in degrees of the angles of a triangle is 180.

4

1

A function f satisfies $f(-1)=-3$ and $f(2)=7$.
A function g satisfies $g(2)=-3$ and $g(7)=-23$.
What is the value of $g(f(2))$?

A) 7

B) -1

C) -3

D) -23

2

$$9x^2+9x-28=0$$

If p and q are two solutions of the equation above, which of the following is the value of $3|p-q|$?

A) 5

B) 8

C) 11

D) 13

3

$$C=3(G-4)$$

The formula above shows how the amount of allowance Cooper gets from his mother, C, in \$, relates to his final grade in his Mathematics class, G, after school's out for summer. Based on the equation, which of the following must be true?

I. If Cooper received \$3 more for his allowance this summer than last summer, then Cooper's final grade for this summer would be 1 point higher than his final grade last summer.

II. If Cooper improves his final grade by 12 points next summer, then the allowance he receives will increase by an additional \$36.

III. If Cooper's allowance for this summer was \$1 lower than last summer's, then Cooper's final grade would have been lower by $\frac{14}{3}$ points this summer compared to last summer.

A) I only

B) II only

C) III only

D) I and II only

4

4

At the Senior School of Josephsaint's Institution, 25 percent of the male students and 30 percent of the female students were chosen to become orientation group leaders (OGLs) in the year 2014. If there were 80 students enrolled at the Senior School of Josephsaint's Institution in 2014 with an equal number of male and female students, which of the following is closest to the total number of male and female students at the Senior School of Josephsaint's Institution who were chosen to become OGLs?

A) 10

B) 15

C) 22

D) 40

5

According to Newton's Second Law, the resultant force of a moving object is given by the product of its mass, in kg, and its acceleration, in ms^{-2}. If a scientist calculates that the resultant force of a toy truck is 2700 kg ms^{-2} and its acceleration is 300 ms^{-2}, what is its mass?

A) $\frac{1}{9}$ kg

B) 9 kg

C) 27 kg

D) 81 kg

Questions 6 and 7 refer to the following information.

Preferences of ice cream flavors in 2011

Age	Chocolate	Vanilla	Strawberry	Total
5–10	265	482	245	992
11–15	462	125	375	962
16–20	175	234	572	981
21–25	196	373	386	955
Total	1098	1214	1578	3890

The table above shows the results of a survey given out to various groups of people in different age groups.

6

What is the probability that someone the age of 14 prefers chocolate ice cream over other flavors?

A) $\frac{231}{481}$

B) $\frac{481}{231}$

C) $\frac{231}{1945}$

D) $\frac{77}{183}$

7

Of the total number of people surveyed, how many people prefer vanilla flavored ice cream? Round to the nearest tenth percent.

A) 25.5%

B) 28.2%

C) 31.2%

D) 39.7%

8

The graph of the linear function g passes through the origin and points (a, b) in the xy-plane. If $a+b=0$, $a \neq b$, which of the following is true about the slope of the graph of g?

A) It is positive.

B) It is negative.

C) It equals 1.

D) It is undefined.

9

Estimated Hours of Sleep per Day of 20 students									
9	9	8.5	8	8	7.5	7.5	7	7	7
7	7	7	6.5	6.5	6.5	6	5.5	5.5	5

The table above shows the estimated hours of sleep per day of 20 students. What is the value of x if x is equal to $\dfrac{2}{5}$ of the mean of the values listed above?

A) 2.82

B) 7.05

C) 20

D) 141

Questions 10 and 11 refer to the following information.

Age	Ticket Price
Under 5	$6.89
Over 6 Under 18	$8.99
Over 19 Under 65	$9.99
Over 66	$7.99

10

Kiara's family of five went to watch a movie, and paid exactly $45.85 total. Three people paid the same price for their tickets, one person paid $6.89, and one person paid $20.98 less than the total price for the three people. What percent of their family is over 19 years old?

A) 40%

B) 60%

C) 80%

D) 100%

11

The next year, the price for people under 18 and over 6 increased by 10%. Compared to the previous year, how much more money does Kiara's family have to pay for their family of five? (Round to the nearest hundredth.)

A) $0.90

B) $1.00

C) $9.89

D) $46.75

12

What is the sum of all values of x that satisfy $5x^2-15x+6=0$?

A) -3

B) $\frac{6}{5}$

C) 2

D) 3

13

Jim is trying to lose weight by having a steady work-out schedule. If his weight decreases at a monthly rate of 2%, and his initial weight is 220lbs, which of the following functions $w(x)$ model Jim's weight 10 months later?

A) $w(10)=220(2)^{10}$

B) $w(10)=220\left(\frac{2}{100}\right)^{10}$

C) $w(10)=220\left(\frac{98}{100}\right)^{10}$

D) $w(10)=220\left(\frac{102}{100}\right)^{10}$

14

In a circle with center O and radius of 6, the area of the sector formed by central angle AOB is 9π. In radians, what is the value of the central angle?

A) $\frac{\pi}{4}$ rad

B) $\frac{\pi}{2}$ rad

C) π rad

D) 9π rad

Questions 15 and 16 refer to the following information.

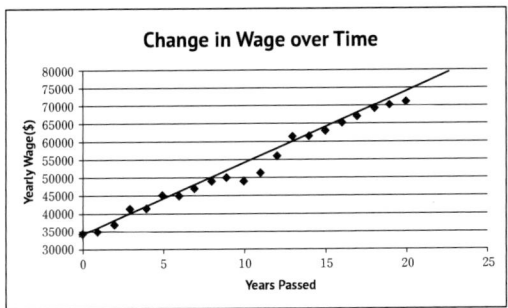

The scatterplot above shows the change in Andy's yearly wage. The line shown indicates the expected wage increase, and has the equation $y = 2000x + 34000$.

15

Which of the following most accurately describe what 34000 represents in the equation and scatterplot given above?

A) The number 34000 represents the rate of change of Andy's monthly wage.

B) The equation and the scatterplot show that 34000 is the yearly wage that Andy received the first year of his job.

C) The number 34000 is the slope of the equation given.

D) The equation shows that the number 34000 is the yearly wage that Andy is to receive after one year has passed.

16

If Andy's wage increases exactly as predicted by the expected wage increase, how much yearly wage would Andy earn after 28 years have passed?

A) $75,000

B) $80,000

C) $85,000

D) $90,000

17
$$x^2 + y^2 - 6x - 4y + 4 = 0$$

The equation above is an equation for a circle in the xy-plane. Which of the following are the coordinates for the center of the circle?

A) $(3, 2)$

B) $(-3, 2)$

C) $(-3, -2)$

D) $(3, -2)$

18

Hydrochloric acid is a strong acid that reacts with metals to form salt and hydrogen. The stronger the concentration of the acid, the faster the rate of reaction. A solution of 1 mol dm^{-3} hydrochloric acid can fully react with 6 strips of magnesium within a minute. If each strip of magnesium weighs $8\frac{1}{4}$ g, what is the total mass of magnesium dissolved, in g, when a solution of 6 mol dm^{-3} is used?

A) 297

B) 152

C) 49.5

D) 36

19

The half-life of a substance refers to the time required for a quantity to reduce to half its initial value. Radium-226, a radioactive isotope of Radium, has a half-life of 1600 years. If there are x grams of Radium-226 initially, which of the following expressions represent the amount of remaining Radium after 4800 years?

A) $x \times \frac{1}{3}$

B) $x \times \left(\frac{1}{2}\right)^3$

C) $x \times 2^3$

D) $x \times 3$

20

If $f(x) = 3x - 11$, what is $f(2x+1)$ equal to?

A) $6x^2 + 3x - 11$

B) $6x - 14$

C) $6x - 8$

D) $6x + 12$

Questions 21 and 22 refer to the following information.

$$F = G\frac{m_1 m_2}{r^2}$$

The gravitational force of attraction, F, existing between two objects with masses m_1 and m_2 and separated by distance r, is given by the formula above. G represents the gravitational constant.

21

Which of the following expresses the distance between two objects in terms of their masses, the force of attraction between them, and the gravitational constant?

A) $r = \sqrt{G\frac{m_1 m_2}{F}}$

B) $r = G\sqrt{\frac{m_1 m_2}{F}}$

C) $r^2 = G\frac{m_1 m_2}{F}$

D) $r^2 = G\frac{F}{m_1 m_2}$

22

A scientist is conducting an experiment in which he measures the gravitational forces of attraction between two weights by varying the distances between them. When the scientist separated them with a distance of x meters, the forces of attraction were 36 times that when the weights were y meters from each other. What is the ratio of y to x?

A) $\frac{1}{6}$

B) $\frac{1}{36}$

C) 6

D) 36

23

What is the product of all values of x that satisfy $3x^2 - 5x + 2 = 0$?

A) $\frac{5}{3}$

B) 1

C) $\frac{2}{3}$

D) $\frac{3}{2}$

Questions 24 and 25 refer to the following information.

$$y = v_0 t - \frac{1}{2} g t^2$$

The equation above expresses the vertical position y of a ball at time t thrown upwards from the ground with an initial velocity of v_0 from the ground. ($g = 9.8 \text{m/s}^2$)

24

How many seconds will it take for the ball to reach 396.9m above the ground if the initial velocity was 88.2m/s?

A) 5

B) 7

C) 9

D) 11

25

If the ball was 34.3m above the ground 7 seconds after being thrown upwards, what is the initial velocity of the ball?

A) 4.9 m/s

B) 9.8 m/s

C) 19.6 m/s

D) 39.2 m/s

26

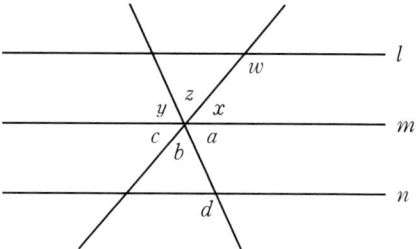

In the figure above, lines l, m, and n are parallel. If $y = z$, which of the following must be true?

I. $w = 2y$
II. $d = x + y$
III. $c = y$
IV. $b = y$

A) II, III, and IV only

B) I, II, and III only

C) I, II, and IV only

D) I, III, and IV only

27

$$x = 2y + 1$$
$$3xy = 4y + 5$$

If $y > 0$ in the system of equations above, what is the value of $x - y$?

A) 1

B) 2

C) 3

D) 4

28

x	-3	-2	-1	0	1	2
y	$\frac{11}{2}$	3	$\frac{3}{2}$	1	$\frac{3}{2}$	3

The table above shows some values of the function $f(x)$. Which of the following defines $f(x)$?

A) x^2+2

B) $\frac{x^2}{2}$

C) $\frac{x^2+2}{2}$

D) None of the above

29

If $10x-2=-10$, find the value of $-20x-5$.

A) -21

B) -16

C) 11

D) 16

30

If $y=kx$, where k is a constant, and $y=12$ when $x=72$, what is the value of y when $x=42$?

A) -22

B) 6

C) 7

D) 252

4

DIRECTIONS

For questions 31-38, solve the problem and enter your answer in the grid, as described below, on the answer sheet.

1. Although not required, it is suggested that you write your answer in the boxes at the top of the columns to help you fill in the circles accurately. You will receive credit only if the circles are filled in correctly.

2. Mark no more than one circle in any column.

3. No question has a negative answer.

4. Some problems may have more than one correct answer. In such cases, grid only one answer.

5. **Mixed numbers** such as $3\frac{1}{2}$ must be gridded as 3.5 or 7/2. (If $3\,1\,/\,2$ is entered into the grid, it will be interpreted as $\frac{31}{2}$, not $3\frac{1}{2}$.)

6. **Decimal answers**: If you obtain a decimal answer with more digits than the grid can accommodate, it may be either rounded or truncated, but it must fill the entire grid.

Answer: $\frac{7}{12}$ Answer: 2.5

Acceptable ways to grid $\frac{2}{3}$ are:

Answer: 201 - either position is correct.

NOTE: You may start your answer in any column, space permitting. Columns you don't need to use should be left blank.

CONTINUE

Questions 31 and 32 refer to the following information.

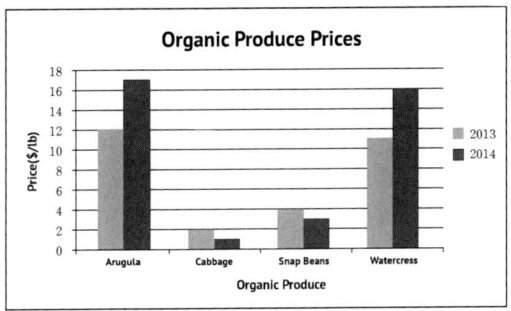

The chart above shows the prices of various organic produce, for the years 2013 and 2014.

31

If the data from the year 2013 is plotted along the x−axis of a scatterplot, and the data from the year 2014 is plotted along the y−axis, how many data points would be above the line $y=x$?

32

What is the percent increase of watercress prices from 2013 to 2014? Round to the nearest tenth.

33

Sean observed a random sample of his schoolmates and categorized them into two groups: Those with straight hair, and those with curly hair. Of the 120 students he observed, 31.7% had curly hair. Based on this information, about how many students in a lecture hall full of 315 students may be expected to have straight hair? (Round to the nearest whole number.)

Questions 34 and 35 refer to the following information.

	Scores	
Exam	Student A	Student B
Test 1	92	77
Test 2	86	83
Test 3	75	67
Test 4	98	71
Homework	76	
Total		

The table above shows the tests and homework scores of students A and B. All of the tests and homework are weighted equally.

34

What is Student A's average score? Round to the nearest tenth.

35

If the students need an average of at least 75 to pass, what is the minimum score Student B needs for homework in order to pass?

36

The abyssal zone is a zone of the ocean between 13,123 feet and 19,685 feet below sea level. At a depth of 13,123 feet below sea level, the pressure in the abyssal zone is 5,766 pounds per square inches (psi), and at a depth of 19,685 feet below sea level, the pressure in the abyssal zone is 8,649 psi. For every additional 33 feet away from the sea level, the pressure increases by p psi, where p is a constant. What is the value of p, rounded to the nearest tenth?

4

Questions 37 and 38 refer to the following information.

Class	Number of Students		Total
	Females	Males	
Chemistry	19	14	
Biology		9	
Physics	14		
Total		41	

37

How many male students are there in Physics class?

38

If the total number of students in Biology class is equal to $\frac{2}{3}$ of the total number of students in Chemistry class, how many students are there in total?

STOP

If you finish before time is called, you may check your work on this section only.
Do not turn to any other section.

No Test Material On This Page

Answer Sheet

Part 3

SAT® Practice Test #1
Answers and Explanations

ANSWER KEY

READING TEST

1. C	14. C	27. C	40. D
2. C	15. A	28. C	41. A
3. A	16. C	29. D	42. C
4. B	17. C	30. A	43. B
5. A	18. A	31. D	44. B
6. D	19. D	32. D	45. A
7. A	20. A	33. C	46. A
8. D	21. D	34. A	47. B
9. C	22. B	35. D	48. A
10. D	23. C	36. D	49. C
11. C	24. A	37. C	50. C
12. C	25. D	38. C	51. D
13. B	26. B	39. D	52. A

WRITING AND LANGUAGE TEST

1. C	12. B	23. A	34. C
2. A	13. C	24. D	35. D
3. C	14. B	25. B	36. A
4. B	15. D	26. C	37. C
5. D	16. C	27. A	38. A
6. A	17. D	28. C	39. D
7. B	18. B	29. A	40. C
8. C	19. D	30. A	41. A
9. C	20. C	31. A	42. C
10. A	21. B	32. A	43. D
11. B	22. A	33. B	44. D

MATH – NO CALCULATOR

1. D	6. C	11. C	16. 40
2. B	7. D	12. A	17. 5/13
3. B	8. D	13. B	18. 1
4. D	9. A	14. A	19. 4/19
5. C	10. D	15. A	20. 1670

MATH – CALCULATOR

1. D	11. A	21. A	31. 2
2. C	12. D	22. C	32. 45.5
3. D	13. C	23. C	33. 215
4. C	14. B	24. C	34. 85.4
5. B	15. B	25. D	35. 77
6. A	16. D	26. C	36. 14.5
7. C	17. A	27. B	37. 18
8. B	18. A	28. C	38. 87
9. A	19. B	29. C	
10. B	20. C	30. C	

Practice Test 1

Answers and Explanations

Section 1. Reading Test

Passage I

Passage Summary

Lines

1-11: A Sergey is talking to himself, practicing what he will say when he proposes to Varenka.

12-41: They are in the woods, gathering mushrooms with some children. She is aware that there is a chance Sergey might propose to her. He is aware that she is aware, and they are both excited as they continue to gather mushrooms.

42-53: Despite their excitement, both of them are having difficulty finding the strength to speak or act as they would like. Their nervousness makes them do and say things that make the romance of the moment diminish. Sergey is annoyed that she talks about unrelated, unimportant things, and she is nervous, so she talks about unimportant things.

54-65: Varenka is very excited at the idea of marrying a man like Sergey and expects that his proposal will come at any moment.

66-77: He is so aware of her awareness of his intention that he feels sorry for making her feel nervous, and he hesitates.

78-88: In his hesitation, he says something trivial about the differences between types of mushrooms and it sucks the romance and feeling out of the moment, and Sergey does not propose.

89-100: Despite their mutual disappointment, they are both somewhat relieved that nothing happened. They go back to playing with the children. Sergey later rationalizes his lack of action with the idea that he should stay true to his late wife.

Main Idea

Sergey wants to propose to Varenka in the woods. Varenka knows it, and Sergey knows she knows it. They are both excited, but their mutual anticipation makes the whole thing fall apart. However, they are both fine with the outcome.

Tone

Slightly melancholy, humorous

Vocabulary & Phrases

Line	Word/Phrase		Meaning
Line 6	offer you my hand		청혼하다
Line 8	paces	n.	걸음, 보폭
Line 19	kerchief	n.	(목이나 머리에 두르는) 스카프
Line 23	throng	v.	(떼를 지어) 모여있다
Line 24	twig	n.	(나무의) 잔가지
Line 25	fungus	n.	균류, 곰팡이류. 여기서는 버섯을 가리킴
Line 26	rosy	a.	발그레한, 붉은 빛을 띤
Line 27	thrust itself	v.	밀치다, 밀어붙이다
Line 25	split in half across its rosy cap by the dry grass from under which it thrust itself		마른 풀 아래에서 버섯이 뚫고 나오면서, 마른 풀 때문에 붉은 빛을 띤 버섯의 갓(cap)이 반으로 갈라진 모습을 말함
Line 34	faint	a.	(동사 feel과 같이 써서) 실신할 것 같은, 어지러운
Line 47	utter	v.	말을 하다, 언급하다
Line 51	edible	a.	먹을 수 있는
Line 52	principally	adv.	주로, mainly
Line 56	throb	v.	고동치다, 울리다
Line 64	frightened	a.	무서워하는, 두려운
Line 64	dread	v.	두려워하다
Line 68	flushed	a.	(사람의 얼굴이) 빨간, 상기된
Line 68	downcast	a.	(눈을) 내리뜬
Line 69	betray	v.	(적에게 정보를) 넘겨주다; 여기서는 감정을 무심코 노출시키다, 드러내다라는 뜻으로 쓰였다.
Line 71	slight	n.	모욕, 무시
Line 72	ran over all the arguments in support of his decision		그의 결정을 지지해 줄 수 있는 근거(가 될만한 것들)를 살펴보았다
Line 76	reflection	n.	생각
Line 78	birch	n.	자작나무
Line 80	quiver	v.	(가볍게) 떨리다
Line 83	stalk	n.	(식물의) 줄기
Line 88	subside	v.	가라앉다, 진정되다
Line 93	unconsciously	adv.	무의식적으로
Line 95	sore	a.	화끈거리는; 감정이 상한
Line 100	be false to		~을 배반하다, ~에 대해 불성실하다

Question Explanations

Q1 Question Type: Purpose

Answer Key : (C)

The first sentence shows how Sergei views Varenka ("the ideal of the woman I loved and should be happy to call my wife"). This is also the reason why he approaches Varenka following this speech. Hence, the answer is (C) establish the speaker's motivation regarding another character.

Eliminate

(A) This is less Sergey's concrete plan for the future than a loose image he set for himself in the past
(B) This is not an "initial conversation"; Sergei is talking to himself
(D) Sergei's words are consistent with his emotional state

Q2 Question Type: Detail

Answer Key : (C)

As can be seen from "woman…happy to call my wife…met what I sought-in you" (line 2-5), Sergei views Varenka as someone he wishes to marry. Hence, the answer is (C) a potential spouse.

Key Point

ideal of a woman I loved and should be happy to call my wife (lines 2-3) = potential spouse

Eliminate

(A) Not mentioned
(B) "intimidating" is too strong
(D) Evidence that Sergey is a "nature enthusiast" is not mentioned

Q3 Question Type: Line evidence

Answer Key : (A)

Find the lines where the answer for question number 2 can be found. Lines 1-6 show that Sergey sees Varenka as someone he wishes to marry. Hence, the answer is (A).

Eliminate

(B), (C), (D) Keywords related to "a potential spouse" are not mentioned

Q4 Question Type: Inference

Answer Key : (B)

As can be seen from "Varenka saw that he wanted to speak; she guessed of what, and felt faint with joy and panic" (line 33-34), Varenka already suspects Sergey's intentions and is anticipating his words. However, as can be seen from "she was almost certain she was in love with him. And this moment it would have to be decided. She felt frightened" (lines 61-64), even though Varenka is almost sure she loves Sergey, she isn't a hundred percent sure of her emotions and fears making a decision. Hence, the answer is (B) eager anticipation of intentions mixed with a lack of confidence.

Key Point

saw that he wanted to speak; she guessed of what (lines 33-34) = anticipation
almost certain (line 62), frightened (line 64) = lack of confidence

Eliminate

(A) "advance to a higher social standing" is not mentioned

(C) "reluctance toward the potential marriage" is not mentioned

(D) "shameful acceptance" is not mentioned

Q5 Question Type: Purpose

Answer Key : (A)

As can be seen from "But against her own will, as it were accidentally, Varenka said:" (lines 40-41) and "but instead of those words, some utterly unexpected reflection that occurred to him made him ask:" (lines 75-77), Varenka and Sergey both bring up the subject of mushrooms to avoid Sergey's proposal for marriage. Hence, the answer is (A) They are used by the characters to avoid speaking of a momentous subject.

Eliminate

(B), (C) Not true for Sergey

(D) "social convention" is not mentioned

Q6 Question Type: Purpose

Answer Key : (D)

As can be seen from "After a silence it would have been easier for them to say what they wanted say than after talking about mushrooms" (lines 38-40), the subject of mushrooms only makes it harder for Sergey to bring up the subject of marriage. Hence, the answer is (D) making it more difficult for Sergey to broach the topic on his mind.

Key Point

it would have been easier (line 38) = making it more difficult

Eliminate

(A) There is no flow of conversation, only silence

(B) Sergey has not proposed yet

(C) "delicate subject" is not mentioned

Q7 Question Type: Line evidence

Answer Key : (A)

Find the lines where the answer for question 6 can be found. Lines 36-40 show that the subject of mushrooms only makes it harder for Sergey to propose. Hence, the answer is (A).

Eliminate

(B) Keywords related to "the topic on his mind" are not mentioned

(C), (D) Keywords related to "mushrooms" are not mentioned

Q8 Question Type: Inference

Answer Key : (D)

As can be seen from "He could not be false to the memory of Marie" (line 99-100), Sergey decides that his decision to propose to Veranka goes against the memory of his late wife. Hence, the answer is (D) faithless to his past.

Key Point

false to the memory of Marie (line 100) = faithless to his past

Eliminate

(A) Sergey's intentions were never actually executed

(B) "deluded" is too strong

(C) "setting" is not mentioned

Q9 Question Type: Inference

Answer Key : (C)

As can be seen from "she guessed of what, and felt faint with joy and panic" (lines 33-34) and "the flushed cheeks and the downcast eyes of Varenka betrayed a painful suspense" (lines 68-69), Varenka initially feels nervous and excited about Sergey's possible proposal. However, as can be seen from "Varenka felt both sore and ashamed; at the same time she had a sense of relief" (lines 95-96), when Sergey fails to propose, Varenka feels both shame and relief. Hence, the answer is (C) nervous excitement about a possible proposal to relief and shame over its failure.

Key Point

joy and panic (line 34), painful suspense (line 69) = nervous excitement

sore and ashamed (line 95), sense of relief (line 96) = relief and shame

Eliminate

(A) "future change in position" and "situational difficulties" are not mentioned

(B) "anxiety over her future" is not mentioned

(D) "self-blame" is not mentioned

Q10 Question Type: Main idea

Answer Key : (D)

The entire passage is about how Sergey tries to bring up the subject of marriage to Veranka. However, as can be seen from lines 42-50 and lines 77-88, the recurring subject of mushrooms makes him give up his attempt to propose. Hence, the answer is (D) A character plans to make a proposal of marriage, but gives up when an irrelevant subject diverts him.

Eliminate

(A) Sergey brings up the memory of Marie only after he gets back home and goes over the whole day in his head

(B) Marriage never actually surfaces as a subject of conversation, "original" or otherwise

(C) "humiliation" is too strong; also, Veranka is relieved at the same time that she feels ashamed

Passage II

Passage Summary

Lines

1-10: Don't worry about what other people are thinking; it will only distract you from what you want.

11-25: Keep your thoughts focused and appropriate, so that you would be able to answer the question "What are you thinking?" honestly, openly, and without shame. This will prove beneficial to you socially.

26-38: Anyone who can do this will be safe from most social and mental harm; pay attention to the motivations of others in extreme circumstances only.

39-50: Accept and be grateful for what you have, because everyone only gets what they are given in life and is responsible for what they have. They should only care about people who also care about things in this way.

51-58: The best kind of person will ignore praise from people who don't follow this advice because such individuals can't judge themselves, let alone others.

Main Idea

Don't worry about what other people think, make sure what you think about is worth thinking about, and don't think about things you don't have. Anyone who chooses not to think this way isn't worth your while.

Tone

Instructive, imperative

Vocabulary & Phrases

Line 1	remainder	n.	나머지
Line 8	contrive	v.	(어떻게든) ~하다
Line 14	malignant	a.	(악성) 종양
Line 20	benevolent	a.	자애로운
Line 24	suspicion	n.	혐의, 의혹, 의심
Line 25	blush	v.	얼굴이 빨개지다
Line 29	deity	n.	신
Line 30	uncontaminated	a.	오염되지 않은
Line 31	insult	n.	모욕적인 말이나 행동
Line 33	dyed	a.	물든, 염색된
Line 41	allotted	a.	할당된

Question Explanations

Q11 Question Type: Main idea

Answer Key : (C)

As can be seen from "Do not waste the remainder of your life in thoughts about others" (line 1-2), Aurelius believes that people should think about themselves and not waste time thinking about others. Also, from "...makes us wander away from the observation of our own driving purpose" (line 9-10), it can be seen that Aurelius believes such thoughts make people forget their own purpose. Hence, the answer is (C) do not assert their own thoughts and beliefs, losing their purpose in life.

Key Point

thoughts about others (line 2) = do not assert their own thoughts and beliefs

wander away from the observation of our own driving purpose (line 9-10) = losing their purpose in life

Eliminate

(A) "egotistic" is not mentioned

(B) "deviate from the banality of the everyday" is not mentioned

(D) "corrupt and inhumane" is not mentioned

Q12 Question Type: Vocabulary in context

Answer Key : (C)

In context, "contriving" is used here with a meaning similar to "thinking" (line 7). Hence, the answer is (C) planning.

Eliminate

(A), (B), (D) Wrong meaning in context

Q13 Question Type: Purpose

Answer Key : (B)

Blushing usually occurs when someone is embarrassed or is ashamed of himself. In this paragraph, "thoughts about pleasure or sensual enjoyments" (line 22-23) and "rivalry or envy and suspicion" (line 23-24) are used as examples of (B) thoughts shameful to oneself.

Eliminate

(A) "rivalry or envy and suspicion" are not "delightful imagination"

(C) "socially benevolent" is not mentioned

(D) "ambiguous" is not mentioned

Q14 Question Type: Vocabulary in context

Answer Key : (C)

In context, "portion" is used here with a meaning similar to "that which has been allotted to himself out of the sum total of things" (line 40-42). Hence, the answer is (C) part of a whole.

Eliminate

(A), (B), (D) Wrong meaning in context

Q15 Question Type: Detail

Answer Key : (A)

As can be seen from "to care for all men is according to man's nature" (line 47-48), Aurelius believes that people should help each other. However, as can be seen from "...not of all, but of those only who attempt to live according to nature" (line 49-50), he also believes that people should care only for those who try to live rationally. Hence, the answer is (A) to support other reasonable people.

Key Point

to care (line 47) = to support

those only who attempt to live according to nature (line 49-50) = reasonable people

Eliminate

(B) "regardless of who they are" is not true

(C) "spiritually enlightened" is not mentioned

(D) "single universal aspiration" is not mentioned

Q16 Question Type: Line evidence

Answer Key : (C)

Find the lines where the answer for question 15 can be found. Lines 46-50 show that Aurelius believes people should help other rational people. Hence, the answer is (C).

Eliminate

(A), (B), (D) Keywords related to "support other reasonable people" are not mentioned

Q17 Question Type: Inference

Answer Key : (C)

Look at line 51: "But as to those who do not live so". It can be assumed from this line that the "men" are people who do not live according to Aurelius' previous guideline, one part of which is that "We ought then to check in the series of our thoughts everything that is without a purpose and useless" (line 11-13). Thus, the "men" are those without purpose and useful thoughts. Also, from "they are not even satisfied with themselves" (line 57-58), it can be seen that the "men" are also insecure. Hence, the answer is (C) insecure beings who do not have their own thoughts and purpose in life.

Key Point

not even satisfied with themselves (line 57-58) = insecure

everything that is without a purpose and useless (line 12-13) = do not have their own thoughts and purpose in life

Eliminate

(A) This is Aurelius' ideal man

(B) "average" is not mentioned

(D) "distrustful" is not mentioned

Q18 Question Type: Detail

Answer Key : (A)

As can be seen from "and he is persuaded that his own portion is good" (line 43), Aurelius claims that a person who owns his own life and thoughts is satisfied with what he already has. In other words, he is content with this life. Also, as can be seen from "it is only what belongs to him that he uses as a motivation" (line 39-40), the person is also motivated by what he has and tries to do his best with it. Hence, the answer is (A) content with his life and makes the most out of it.

Key Point

persuaded that his own portion is good (line 43) = content with his life

uses as a motivation (line 39-40) = makes the most out of it

Eliminate

(B) "willing to go beyond" is not mentioned

(C) "dissatisfied" is not true

(D) not mentioned

Q19 Question Type: Line evidence

Answer Key : (D)

Find the lines where the answer for question 18 can be found. Lines 39-46 show that a person who owns his own life and thoughts will be satisfied with that life and make the most out it. Hence, the answer is (D).

Eliminate

(A), (B) Keywords related to "content with his life" are not mentioned

(C) These lines are describing a person who owns his own life and thoughts, not what he does

Q20 Question Type: Main idea

Answer Key : (A)

On the one hand, "with perfect openness one can immediately answer "This or That", and from what you say it will be plain that everything about you is simple and benevolent" (line 17-20) represents thoughts that Aurelius believes to be appropriate. On the other hand, "anything else that would make you blush if you said you were thinking about it" (line 24-25), as explained in question 13, represents thoughts that Aurelius believes to be inappropriate and shameful. Hence, the second paragraph is trying to set up a contrast between (A) appropriate thoughts and inappropriate thoughts.

Key Point

with perfect openness one can immediately answer "This or That" (line 17-18) = appropriate thoughts

anything else that would make you blush if you said you were thinking about it (line 24-25) = inappropriate thoughts

Eliminate

(B) "rational people and irrational people" are not mentioned in the second paragraph

(C) "malevolence" is too narrow; not every thought mentioned can be categorized as malevolent

(D) the term "social animal" (line 21) is used here to refer to a human, not an actual animal

Passage III

Passage Summary

Lines

1-8: It's disappointing that the high speed rail system built in California is so expensive and slow, especially since there are such good tech companies there.

8-19: Sure, we need alternatives to driving and flying, but if they aren't better, they aren't really alternatives.

19-32: Any possible option needs to fit many criteria of safety and efficiency, but there is nothing in development that meets these criteria.

33-53: For anything longer than 900 miles, a plane makes sense, but under 900 miles you are just taking off and landing the whole time. To go fast, you need to go high where air pressure is low, since it gets in your way.

54-66: Hyperloop would be a special tube containing a special environment to keep the air pressure low, like in old pneumatic tubes. This could allow high speed travel.

67-82: Pushing all the air in the tube is nearly impossible because of friction. Taking all the air out would be nearly impossible to achieve on a regular basis.

82-86: Thus, maintaining a very low pressure environment would be the best way to go.

Main Idea

There are a lot of difficulties with high-speed travel. However, a low pressure tube might be a good solution over certain distances. This idea poses its own challenges, though.

Tone

Matter-of-fact, informative

Vocabulary & Phrases

Line 5	index	v.	색인을 만들어 정리하다
Line 6	rover	n.	방랑자; 여기서는 화성 탐사선을 말함
Line 9	statewide	a.	(미국에서) 주 전체에 걸친
Line 9	mass transit	n.	대량수송수단
Line 11	alternative	n.	대안
Line 14	unsubsidized	a.	보조금을 받지 않은
Line 15	orders of magnitude	n.	자릿수 (두 자릿수, 세 자릿수 등으로 표현되는)
Line 18	by rights	adv.	원칙적으로(ideally)
Line 21	immune	a.	면역성이 있는; ~에 영향을 받지 않는
Line 21	sustainably	adv.	지속적으로
Line 23	disruptive	a.	지장을 주는
Line 26	criteria	n.	기준

Line 26	implement	v.	시행하다
Line 29	let alone		~하기는커녕, ~은 고사하고
Line 30	robust	a.	튼튼한, 탄탄한
Line 32	fruition	n.	(계획, 과정, 활동의) 성과, 결실
Line 37	inflection point	n.	변곡점
Line 37	supersonic	a.	음속의
Line 42	showstopper	n.	하드웨어나 소프트웨어를 못 쓰게 만드는 버그
Line 45	infrastructure	n.	사회(공공기반)시설
Line 47	pointless	a.	무의미한, 할 가치가 없는
Line 50	density	n.	밀도
Line 51	exponentially	adv.	기하급수적으로
Line 52	molasses	n.	당밀; 아주 걸쭉한 시럽
Line 53	velocity	n.	속도
Line 55	teleportation	n.	순간이동
Line 59	tricky	a.	까다로운, 힘든
Line 60	extreme	n.	극단적인 것
Line 61	pneumatic	a.	공기가 가득 찬
Line 65	propel	v.	(몰거나 밀거나 해서) 나아가게 하다
Line 65	pod	n.	꼬투리; 유선형의 공간, 장비, 또는 탈 것
Line 67	friction	n.	마찰, 저항
Line 70	stupendous	a.	엄청나게 큰, 거대한
Line 72	hard vacuum		강력한 진공(상태)
Line 74	electromagnetic	a.	전자기의
Line 74	suspension	n.	서스펜션 (자동차에서 차체의 무게를 받쳐주는 장치)
Line 79	leaky seal		밀봉이 되지 않아 새는
Line 86	inherently	adv.	본질적으로

Question Explanations

Q21 Question Type: Vocabulary in context

Answer Key : (D)

At this point, the passage is discussing a hypothetical train that could be a potential "alternative to flying or driving" (line 11); the phrase "in question" (line 13) serves to emphasize that it is this "train" we are currently discussing and considering. Hence, the answer is (D) consideration.

Eliminate

(A), (B), (C) Wrong meaning in context

Q22 Question Type: Main idea

Answer Key : (B)

As can be seen from "Compared to the alternatives, it should ideally be: safer, faster, lower cost, more convenient, immune to weather, sustainably self-powering, resistant to earthquakes, and not disruptive to those along the route" (line 19-23), the author lists the various ways "a new transportation system" (line 17-18) should be better than existing ones. This is the central idea of the first paragraph. The description of the new bullet train is used as an example of a system that does not meet this criteria. Hence, the answer is (B) a new mode of transportation should be superior to the existing ones in every aspect.

Key Point

alternatives (line 19) = existing ones

safer, faster, lower cost, more convenient, immune to weather, sustainably self-powering, resistant to earthquakes, and not disruptive to those along the route (line 20-23) = superior...in every aspect

Eliminate

(A) Not the central idea. Also, the author disapproves of the new "high speed" rail for a number of reasons, not just the cost

(C) Not the central idea

(D) "maintain its popularity" is not mentioned

Q23 Question Type: Line evidence

Answer Key : (C)

Find the lines where the answer for question 22 can be found. Lines 19-24 show that a new mode of transportation should be superior to existing alternatives in every aspect. Hence, the answer is (C).

Eliminate

(A), (B), (D) Keywords related to "superior" are not mentioned

Q24 Question Type: Detail

Answer Key : (A)

As can be seen from "the sonic boom noise on the ground would be no louder than current airliners, so that isn't a showstopper" (line 39-42), the author believes that the relative noiselessness of a supersonic plane is one of its advantages. He further emphasizes this point by referring to it as "a quiet supersonic plane" (line 42). Hence, the answer is (A) Noiselessness.

Key Point

noise on the ground would be no louder than current airliners (line 40-41), quiet (line 42) = noiselessness

Eliminate

(B) "Accessibility" is not mentioned

(C) "Safety" is not mentioned

(D) "Resistance to natural disasters" is not mentioned

Q25 Question Type: Line evidence

Answer Key : (D)

Find the lines where the answer for question 24 can be found. Lines 38-42 mention noiselessness as one of the advantages of a supersonic plane. Hence, the answer is (D).

Eliminate

(A), (B), (C) Keywords related to "Noiselessness" are not mentioned

Q26 Question Type: Vocabulary in context

Answer Key : (B)

From phrases such as "in my opinion" (line 33-34) and the author's unwillingness or inability to quote an exact figure in "high enough altitude and the right geometry" (line 39), it can be assumed that the author is also making a guess about supersonic air travel. Hence, the answer is (B) conjecture.

Key Point

opinion (line 34) = conjecture

Eliminate

(A), (C), (D) Wrong meaning in context

Q27 Question Type: Purpose

Answer Key : (C)

In the previous two paragraphs, the author describes two different transportation systems: "'high speed' rail" (line 1) and "supersonic air travel" (line 37-38). Moreover, as can be seen from "most expensive per mile and one of the slowest in the world" (line 7-8) and "for a sub several hundred mile journey, having a supersonic plane is rather pointless" (line 45-47), he also describes why these two systems cannot be the new mode of transportation. Then, as can be seen from "the only option for super fast travel" (line 57) and "potential solutions" (line 60), the third paragraph introduces the concept of Hyperloop as an alternative solution to the issue of a new transportation system. Hence, the answer is (C) It illustrates a concept that could potentially solve the issue discussed in the first two paragraphs of the passage.

Key Point

"Hyperloop" (line 54) = concept
"super fast travel" (line 57) = issue
"potential solutions" (line 60) = potentially solve

Eliminate

(A) "alternative" is not mentioned
(B) "denounced" is not true
(D) "subsequently argued against" is not true

Q28 Question Type: Inference

Answer Key : (C)

As can be seen from "impossible for all practical purposes" (line 70-71), the author is describing why Hyperloop as of yet cannot become a reality. Hence, the answer is (C).

Key Point

impossible for all practical purposes (line 70-71) = only a conceptual transportation system

Eliminate

(A), (B), (D) The reason Hyperloop is only conceptual right now is not mentioned

Q29 Question Type: Chart

Answer Key : (D)

Look at the graph comparing the estimated speed of High Speed Rail and Hyperloop. The estimated speed of Hyperloop, 800mph, is over three times greater than the estimated speed of High Speed Rail, which is 200mph. Hence, the answer is (D) The Hyperloop is over three times faster than California High Speed Rail.

Eliminate

(A) "very fast" is not supported by the graphs

(B) "distance" is not shown in the graphs

(C) "available" is not true; Hyperloop doesn't exist yet

Q30 Question Type: Chart

Answer Key : (A)

Look at the graph comparing nonstop traveling time from LA to San Francisco for High Speed Rail and Hyperloop. The time for Hyperloop, 25 minutes, is much less than the time for High Speed Rail, which is over 150 minutes. Also, the graph comparing the estimated cost of the two transportation methods also shows that Hyperloop is cheaper to build than the High Speed Rail. In all aspects, the graphs show that Hyperloop is a better transportation method than High Speed Rail. Hence, the answer is (A) The Hyperloop is a better transportation method than high speed railway for cities that are less than 900 miles apart.

Eliminate

(B) "out there" is not true; Hyperloop doesn't exist yet

(C) "air travel" is not mentioned in the graphs

(D) "super quiet tube" is not mentioned in either the passage or the graphs

Q31 Question Type: Chart

Answer Key : (D)

Look at the three graphs. Hyperloop is much cheaper than High Speed Rail, but is faster and requires less traveling time. Hence, the answer is (D) Compared to the California high speed rail, it is more cost-efficient in terms of speed and traveling time.

Eliminate

(A) "extremely low" is too strong. Also, Hyperloop's "quality of speed" is very high

(B), (C) Hyperloop's "traveling time" is much shorter than High Speed Rail's. For transportation, shorter travel time is equal to higher efficiency

Passage IV

Passage Summary

Lines

1-6: Everyone loves the Grand Canyon, especially Americans.

7-17: Formed over a really long time, it is truly impressive.

18-26: The Colorado River formed it and runs through it to this day.

27-50: It is unique among natural sights in that it is oriented downwards; the effect is very powerful indeed!

51-61: It is so amazing you will wonder how it was made. While we can't be entirely sure, geologists have a pretty good guess.

62-75: You can see four layers of rock in the canyon. The top levels were "shaved off", presumably by a glacier, at which point the Colorado River began carving into the rocks below.

76-83: The canyon is still unfinished, as all water that comes through the canyon leaves its own marks.

Main Idea

The Grand Canyon is a magnificent place to visit. Its origin is not one hundred percent known but there is a good hypothesis. The canyon is still changing infinitesimally each year.

Tone

Informative, friendly, impressed

Vocabulary & Phrases

Line 3	flock	v.	떼 지어 가다
Line 9	chasm	n.	(땅, 바위, 얼음 등의 속에 생긴) 아주 깊은 틈, 구멍
Line 12	granite	n.	화강암
Line 12	gorge	n.	협곡
Line 14	erosive	a.	부식성의, 침식에 의한
Line 16	imperceptibly	adv.	인지하지 못한 채, 알지 못하는 사이에
Line 18	drain	v.	(~을 따라) 흘러가다
Line 22	junction	n.	(강의) 합류지점, 연결점
Line 23	tide-water	n.	해안지대
Line 24	headlong	adv.	(머리부터) 거꾸로, 곤두박질쳐서
Line 25	torrent	n.	급류
Line 26	tinted	a.	(~한) 색을 띤
Line 27	a railroad running to the rim		협곡의 가장자리를 따라 가설되어 있는 철도를 가리킴
Line 31	trough	n.	여물통; (산등성이 사이의) 골짜기
Line 34	come upon it unawares		(계획하지 않았는데) 뜻밖에 그것에 부딪히다, 맞닥뜨리다
Line 35	timbered	a.	나무로 지은, 목재의

Line 35	plateau	n.	고원
Line 37	trail	n.	자취, 흔적
Line 39	vista	n.	(아름다운) 경치, 풍경
Line 40	glimpse	n.	잠깐, 언뜻 보는 것
Line 43	haze	n.	연무, 실안개
Line 45	butte	n.	(꼭대기가 평평한) 외딴 산, 언덕
Line 46	minaret	n.	(회교 사원에서 볼 수 있는) 뾰족탑
Line 46	battlement	n.	(총 쏘는 구멍이 나 있는) 흉벽
Line 47	myriad	a.	무수히 많은
Line 47	hue	n.	빛깔, 색조
Line 49	awe	v.	경외심을 갖게 하다
Line 59	layer-cake	n.	여러 층으로 만든 케이크
Line 76	cracking	n.	(무엇이 벌어져서 생긴) 금

Question Explanations

Q32 Question Type: Detail

Answer Key : (D)

As can be seen from "it is still being deepened and widened imperceptibly year by year" (line 15-17), the Grand Canyon's depth and width are increasing anually, or (D) increasingly very slightly each year.

Key Point

deepened and widened imperceptibly year by year (line 15-17) = depth and width of the Grand Canyon are increasing very slightly each year

Eliminate

(A) "there is no other chasm in the world worthy to be compared with it" (line 9-10)
(B) Though the canyon was "created ages and ages ago by the erosive action of water, wind, and frost" (line 14-15), it is still growing
(C) "even more impressive" is not mentioned

Q33 Question Type: Line evidence

Answer Key : (C)

Find the lines where the answer for question 32 can be found. Lines 13-17 show that the depth and width of the Grand Canyon are increasing slightly each year. Hence, the answer is (C).

Eliminate

(A), (B), (D) Keywords related to "increasing" are not mentioned

Q34 Question Type: Vocabulary in context

Answer Key : (A)

Judging from the context, "dashes" is used here with a meaning similar to "flowing" (line 23); the word "torrent" (line 25) refers to a "rapid current", so we can assume that "dashes" means 'flowing rapidly'. Hence, the answer is (A) rushes.

Eliminate

(B), (C), (D) Wrong meaning in context

Q35 Question Type: Purpose

Answer Key : (D)

As can be seen from "No wonder that the first look often awes the spectator into silence and tears!" (line 48-50), the author has the utmost regard for the Grand Canyon. The whole paragraph, from "Imagine a gigantic trough…solid granite" (line 31-34) to "The distant rim…sunlight in myriad hues" (line 43-47), depicts the Grand Canyon in vivid details. Hence, the answer is (D) descriptively extol the beauty of a unique landscape.

Key Point

The distant rim…sunlight in myriad hues (line 43-47) = descriptively

No wonder that the first look often awes the spectator into silence and tears! = extol

Grand Canyon = unique landscape

Eliminate

(A) "geographic composition" is not mentioned

(B) "contrast" is not the primary purpose of the paragraph; the view of the Canyon from the bottom is mentioned only briefly

(C) "importance" is not mentioned

Q36 Question Type: Detail

Answer Key : (D)

As can be seen from "Just between ourselves, no one absolutely can tell just how the miracle occurred" (line 54-55), the origin of the Grand Canyon isn't known exactly. However, as can be seen from "the geologist has put together, bit by bit, thousands of facts…it must stand as at least the probable truth" (line 56-61), thorough collection of information has yielded a convincing hypothesis. Hence, the answer is (D) cannot be definitely ascertained, but can be accurately conjectured through careful study.

Key Point

no one absolutely can tell (line 54-55) = cannot be definitely ascertained

probable truth (line 61) = accurately conjectured

thousands of facts (line 57) = careful study

Eliminate

(A) "universal curiosity" does not pertain to the Grand Canyon's "origin"

(B) "principally due to" is not true

(C) the "transition" occurs from the bottom layer up, not the other way around

Q37 Question Type: Line evidence

Answer Key : (C)

Find the lines where the answer for question 36 can be found. Lines 54-61 show that although no one is absolutely sure how the Grand Canyon originated, there is enough scientific evidence to support a probable hypothesis. Hence, the answer is (C).

Eliminate

(A), (B), (D) Keywords related to "origin" are not mentioned

Q38 Question Type: Vocabulary in context

Answer Key : (C)

From the context clue "convincing" (line 60), it can be assumed that "stand" is used here to mean to "hold" as the "probable truth" (line 61). Hence, the answer is (C) remain valid.

Eliminate

(A), (B), (D) Wrong meaning in context

Q39 Question Type: Chart

Answer Key : (D)

As can be seen from the graph, "Bedrock Failures" takes up only 12% of the sources of debris flow, which is the smallest compared to the other sources of debris flow. Hence, the answer is (D) "Bedrock Failures" is seldom responsible for debris flow.

Eliminate

(A), (B) The "Firehose Effect" takes up the greatest percentage of the sources of debris flow

(C) "rarest" is not mentioned

Q40 Question Type: Chart

Answer Key : (D)

As can be seen from the graph, none of the mentioned sources takes up over 50% of the cause. Hence, the answer is (D) None of the failures causes over half of the debris in the Grand Canyon.

Eliminate

(A) The various failures cause debris flow, not the other way around

(B) The sum of all the percentages amounts to 100%

(C) The "Firehose Effect" leads to more debris flow than "Combination of Failures"

Q41 Question Type: Chart

Answer Key : (A)

As can be seen from the graph, the "Firehose Effect" is the biggest source of debris flow, amounting to 35%. Hence, the answer is (A) the most important source of debris flow in the Grand Canyon.

Eliminate

(B) "least important source" is "Bedrock Failure"

(C) "source of all debris flow" is not true

(D) "residents of the Grand Canyon" are not mentioned

Passage V

Passage 1

Passage Summary

Lines

- **1-6:** Colonization has paid off, but it is too risky to continue.
- **6-15:** All the places left to colonize are either undesirable or are not uncivilized enough. We have been too successful.
- **16-20:** Colonization has been extremely profitable for us.
- **20-26:** However, we have been too aggressive, and now those who are colonized are suspicious of our motives.
- **26-39:** They are starting to question whether the concepts we have been selling them are as good as they appeared at first.
- **40-45:** These concepts are fantastic products, but the ones we export are different than the ones we use at home, apparently.
- **45-55:** The one we ship overseas is pretty on the outside, but empty and horrible inside.
- **56-63:** The "product" of colonization is being harmed by those who are "selling" it without even pretending that it is good; clearly, these new players aren't good at the "game".

Main Idea

Colonization is a lot of empty promises of "civilization" which actually bring only pain and difficulty, and the people who are trying to do it are bad at it.

Tone

Deeply sarcastic, acerbic, brutally critical

Passage 2

Passage Summary

Lines

- **64-77:** We can't just stay in our own borders; since we will have to deal with other countries anyway, we should take control first.
- **78-94:** We defeated tyrants in Manila and Santiago, but if we just leave them alone, they will fall back into anarchy and chaos, allowing others to intervene.
- **95-112:** So, we have a responsibility to take on the task of civilizing these places. It is going to be hard, but we must be strong. We have to set high standards for them and for ourselves.

Main Idea

We have a responsibility to take care of the colonies we took over since they will fall into chaos otherwise. If we don't use our power, someone else will take over anyway.

Tone

Assertive, confident, begrudgingly accepting

Vocabulary & Phrases

Passage 1

Line 6	advisable	a.	바람직한, 권할 만한
Line 6	People that Sit in Darkness		어둠 속에 앉아서 (아무 발언도 하지 않고) 침묵하는 사람들
Line 7	scarce	a.	부족한, 드문
Line 9	indifferent	a.	썩 좋지는 않은, 그저 그런
Line 11	furnish	v.	제공하다, 공급하다
Line 13	injudicious	a.	지혜롭지 못한; 부적절한
Line 15	resolve	n.	(단호한) 결심, 의지
Line 19	sovereignty	n.	통치권
Line 19	emolument	n.	(고소득자에 대한) 보수
Line 21	Christendom	n.	전 세계 기독교
Line 23	stake	n.	지분, 이해관계
Line 37	temperance	n.	절제, 자제
Line 40	bring into camp any idiot sits in darkness anywhere		어떤 바보라도 가만히 침묵하는 무리 안에 받아준다는 뜻
Line 42	adulterate	v.	불순물을 섞다
Line 43	emphatic	a.	단호한, 분명한
Line 50	bale	n.	짐짝, 더미

Passage 2

Line 64	huddle	v.	옹송그리며 모여있다
Line 65	avow	v.	맹세하다
Line 65	assemblage	n.	집합체, 모임
Line 65	well-to-do	a.	부유한, 잘 사는
Line 66	huckster	n.	행상꾼, 보따리장수
Line 67	defeat its own end		그것의 목적에 어긋나다
Line 72	supremacy	n.	패권, 우위, 지상주의

Line 73	isthmian canal	파나마운하
Line 74	vantage	n. 우세, 유리
Line 83	medieval tyranny	중세의 압제
Line 83	savage anarchy	잔인한 무정부상태
Line 88	infamy	n. 악명, 오명
Line 89	wretched	a. 끔찍한, 형편 없는
Line 92	weakling	n. 허약자, 약골
Line 101	vain	a. 헛된, 소용없는
Line 107	grapple	v. 붙잡고 싸우다; (해결책을 찾아) 고심하다
Line 108	rigid accountability	엄격한 의무

Question Explanations

Q42 Question Type: Inference

Answer Key : (C)

As can be seen from "She has been so eager to get every stake that appeared on the green cloth" (line 23-24), the imperialists have been very greedily intruding on their colonies; and as can be seen from "the People who Sit in Darkness have noticed it...and have begun to show alarm. They have become suspicious" (line 24-27), the indigenous people have noticed the imperialists' rapaciousness. Hence, the answer is (C) intrude upon the native population's life in an undesirable way

Key Point

get every stake (line 23) = intrude

People who Sit in Darkness (line 24-25) = native population

suspicious (line 27) = undesirable

Eliminate

(A) "more light than was good for them or profitable for us" (line 11-12)

(B) "boost their economies" is not mentioned

(D) "evangelized" is not mentioned

Q43 Question Type: Line evidence

Answer Key : (B)

Find the lines where the answer for question 42 can be found. Lines 23-29 show that imperialists have been invading on the native population's life in an unfavorable way. Hence, the answer is (B).

Eliminate

(A), (C), (D) Keywords related to "intrude" are not mentioned

Q44 Question Type: Vocabulary in context

Answer Key : (B)

In context, the People that Sit in Darkness were "given" light, albeit more than desirable, from the imperialists. Hence, the answer is (B) provided.

Eliminate

(A), (C), (D) Wrong meaning in context

Q45 Question Type: Detail

Answer Key : (A)

As can be seen from "if we are to hold our own in the struggle for naval and commercial supremacy, we must build up our power without our own borders" (line 70-73), the speaker of Passage 2 believes that in order for a nation to maintain its supremacy over others, it must (A) extend its power and influence overseas.

Key Point

hold our own (line 70-71) = guard its supremacy

build up our power without our own borders (line 72-73) = extend its power and influence overseas

Eliminate

(B) "militarily" is not mentioned

(C) not mentioned

(D) "seize absolute power" is not mentioned

Q46 Question Type: Vocabulary in context

Answer Key : (A)

In context, it can be assumed that "grapple with" is used here with a meaning similar to "face" (line 104); "highest order of integrity and ability" (line 106) indicates that the "new problems" (line 108) that have to be faced will be challenging. Hence, the answer is (A) deal with.

Eliminate

(B), (C), (D) Wrong meaning in context

Q47 Question Type: Detail

Answer Key : (B)

As evinced by "savage anarchy" (line 83) and "utter chaos" (line 89), the speaker believes a country without a leader or a government will collapse. Hence, the answer is (B) be thrown into political turmoil.

Key Point

anarchy (line 84), chaos (line 90) = political turmoil

Eliminate

(A) "economically" is not mentioned

(C) "easily be seized" is not mentioned

(D) "annexed" is not mentioned

Q48 Question Type: Line evidence

Answer Key : (A)

Find the lines where the answer for question 47 can be found. Lines 82-90 show that the speaker believes that if a country becomes leaderless and is left unprovided for, it will fall into political chaos. Hence, the answer is (A).

Eliminate

(B), (C), (D) Keywords related to "political turmoil" are not mentioned

Q49 Question Type: Analyzing multiple texts

Answer Key : (C)

As can be seen in "Some stronger, manlier power would have to step in and do the work" (line 90-91), the author of Passage 2 claims that the nation must intervene overseas for the colony's own good; otherwise, he argues, the colony will fall into chaos. On the other hand, the author of Passage 1 says overseas intervention has only made life more difficult for the indigenous people. Hence, the answer is (C) point out that the nation has failed to live up to its initial intentions regarding overseas intervention given in Passage 2.

Eliminate

(A) "imperialism is necessary for a nation to prosper" is not mentioned in Passage 2
(B) "agree" is not true
(D) Passage 1 does not believe colonialists "support small countries"

Q50 Question Type: Analyzing multiple texts

Answer Key : (C)

Passage 1 talks about the negative aspects of colonialism and argues against it, while Passage 2 discusses reasons colonialism should be carried out. Hence, the answer is (C) Passage 2 presents a different view on an issue discussed in Passage 1.

Eliminate

(A) "same idea" is not true
(B) "more detailed explanation" is not true
(D) "supports" is not true

Q51 Question Type: Inference

Answer Key : (D)

As can be seen from "we must build up our power without our own borders" (line 72-73), the author of Passage 2 calls for overseas expansion. It can therefore be inferred that the United States is aware that its influence can be extended. As for Passage 1, look at "It shows that these new players of it are not sufficiently acquainted with it" (line 61-63). Although the United States is not yet an expert at colonialism, it is still one of the "players", meaning it is at least capable of exerting influence. Hence, the answer is (D) The nation was well aware of the possibility of increasing its international influence.

Eliminate

(A) "Native Americans" are not mentioned in Passage 2
(B) "anti-expansion sentiments" are not mentioned in Passage 2
(C) "fully advocated" is not mentioned in either passage

Q52 Question Type: Analyzing multiple texts

Answer Key : (A)

As can be seen from "We have forgotten our primary goal: to 'face the responsibilities with proper seriousness, courage, and high resolve'" (line 13-15), the author of Passage 1 believes that the United States has failed to properly execute its responsibilities. Hence, the answer is (A) The United States has failed to carry out its duties properly and faithfully as intended.

Key Point

forgotten our primary goal (line 13-14) = failed

face the responsibilities with proper seriousness, courage, and high resolve (line 14-15) = carry out its duties properly and faithfully

Eliminate

(B) Passage 1 is arguing against imperialism itself

(C) "can never benefit" is not supported

(D) "world peace" is not mentioned

Section 2. Writing and Language Test

Q1
Answer: C
Category: Relative Pronouns
Explanation
  C) To create a relative clause about "rates" after the comma, we need to use "which".
Eliminate
  A) run-on, because of the subject "it"
  B) run-on, because of the subject "they"
  D) missing a relative pronoun

Q2
Answer: A
Category: Conjunctive Errors – Adverb Clause
Explanation
  A) "however" is used to contrast the possible solutions presented in the previous sentence with the obstacle in the current sentence.
Eliminate
  B) "Furthermore" is used to advance an argument, not to contrast.
  C) Like "however," "nevertheless" is used to contrast, but it also has the connotation of "anyways," as if to disregard the solutions mentioned in the previous sentence.
  D) "Therefore" is used to logically finish an argument.

Q3
Answer: C
Category: Punctuation
Explanation
  C) There should be no punctuation in "fears of".
Eliminate
  A, B, D) All contain punctuation between "fear" and "of", where there should be none.

Q4
Answer: B
Category: Rhetorical Function
Explanation
  B) The underlined part must connect the two paragraphs. The previous paragraph introduced the problem of too many prisoners. This paragraph presents further obstacles, so "even trickier" underscores the relationship between the two paragraphs.
Eliminate
  A) While "Most of the opposition" does refer to the previous paragraph, in the context of this sentence, the fact that the solutions are closely tied to the local economy does not provide justification for why the opposition is "unreasonable".
  C) While "related" does refer to the previous paragraph, the link between the solution and the local economy cannot be described as merely "interesting".
  D) There is no reference to the previous paragraph here.

Q5
Answer: D
Category: Diction
Explanation
  D) Populations can "provide" labor – which in this context means to suppy prisoners who can offer their services for others.
Eliminate
  A) The populations do not "disseminate" (spread) labor.
  B) The populations do not "bestow" (award) labor, because theirs is not given as a prize.
  C) The populations do not "grant" (allow) labor, because prisoners do not have any such authority.

Q6

Answer: A
Category: Verb Form
Explanation
  A) We know that the infinitive form of the verb "to lower" should be used here because of the word "to" before the underlined portion.
Eliminate
  B, C, D) are not infinitive forms.

Q7

Answer: B
Category: Pronoun, Voice
Explanation
  B) Who is the one "proving" that the environment can influence a person's propensity to crime? It is "These statistics" mentioned in the previous sentence.
Eliminate
  A) "They" refers to the 49% of offenders. The offenders themselves do not prove something, the statistics do.
  C) The word "Those" cannot function as a subject of a verb.
  D) "We" is usually used to refer to the world or a team on whose behalf the author is writing; neither is indicated as proving anything.

Q8

Answer: C
Category: Punctuation, Conjunctive Adverb
Explanation
  C) The key to this question is the punctuation used around "therefore". Choice C correctly isolates "therefore" with a comma without disrupting the flow of the rest of the sentence.
Eliminate
  A) "therefore" cannot come between a prepositional phrase and the independent clause that the prepositional phrase is modifying.
  B) The prepositional phrase appositive must not cut between "need to ensure".
  D) "therefore" is separated from the second sentence by a semicolon, so this does no better job of combining the underlined sentences than how they were originally presented.

Q9

Answer: C
Category: Parallelism
Explanation
  C) "... rate by 23%" should be parallel with "rate by 18%"
Eliminate
  A, B, D) do not achieve any form of parallelism.

Q10

Answer: A
Category: Rhetorical Function
Explanation
  A) The underlined portion anticipates the information that follows, which is that many released convicts end up behind bars again, or "taking paths that will return them to institutions," by calling for preventative measures.
Eliminate
  B, C) no mention of returning to prison
  D) While this choice mentions recommitting crimes, it does not address the main purpose of the support programs mentioned earlier in the sentence, which is prevention.

Q11
Answer : B
Category : Insertion
Explanation
B) Without this sentence, there is only one sentence to conclude the passage, which does not summarize the aforementioned arguments. Insertion is thus necessary for an effective closing.
Eliminate
A) Introducing ideas is not appropriate for the last paragraph of a passage.
C, D) We need to insert this sentence for a summary.

Q12
Answer : B
Category : Redundancy
Explanation
B) This is the only choice without any redundancy.
Eliminate
A) "reiterate" and "repetitively" are redundant.
C) "duplicating" and "over and over again" are redundant.
D) "repetitively" and "replaying" are redundant.

Q13
Answer : C
Category : Verb Form
Explanation
C) The things being cracked are "my fingers and shoulders", by wooden switches.
Eliminate
A) Switches are not the ones being cracked – "my fingers and shoulders" are.
B) "having + past participle" is a dependent clause that requires a comma in front, but there is no comma in front of the underlined portion.
D) The past verb form "cracked" suddenly makes a new independent clause with the subject "switches", but there are no conjunctions to justify this new independent clause.

Q14
Answer : B
Category : Rhetorical Function
Explanation
B) "glissando thumbs" (dragging thumbs rapidly up and down the piano keys), "cramped room" and "cracked fingers and shoulders" suggest that the main reason the author decided to give up music was due to his ailing health.
Eliminate
A) The author did lose enjoyment, but it was not the main reason she quit music, as suggested by the title.
C) There is no mention of any priority other than music in this paragraph.
D) "[my technical skill] came before true success" is nonsensical and not the main point.

Q15
Answer : D
Category : Diction
Explanation
D) Choosing a conjunctive adverb requires analysis of the parts before and after the adverb, which are being linked. Since the author's giving up music is the direct cause of the others' horror, "consequently" is the best adverb to use.
Eliminate
A, B, C) None of these adverbs imply causality.

Q16

Answer : C
Category : Insertion
Explanation

C) The main point in the paragraph is that the parents were severely disappointed in the author. Stating a general statistic about how parents feel about their children's change in major does not help focus on the emotional impact of his parents' disappointment on the author.

Eliminate

A, B) We should not add such a generalizing statement when we are discussing specific characters.

D) A specific claim about the author's parents and not a general claim, was made in the previous sentence.

Q17

Answer : D
Category : Punctuation, Conjunctive Adverb
Explanation

D) The key to this problem is whether "however" belongs to the clause before or after it. Since the author is trying to introduce a bigger problem than her parents' disappointment, "however" belongs to the clause before it.

Eliminate

A, B, C) None of these choices assigns "however" exclusively to the clause preceding the underlined portion.

Q18

Answer : A
Category : Content Order
Explanation

A) Because sentence 2 gives support to the claim in sentence 1 that "music was an object of admiration", it makes sense to leave it where it is.

Eliminate

B) If placed before sentence 1, that would make sentence 2 a topic sentence, but because it contains statistics and examples, it is not fit to be a topic sentence.

C) Placing it after sentence 4 would make it a concluding sentence, but it is better to finish a paragraph with a summary rather than with statistics and examples.

D) Deleting sentence 2 would omit an important support for a claim made in the previous sentence.

Q19

Answer : D
Category : Number Agreement
Explanation

D) "Anyone" is singular.

Eliminate

A,B,C) "survivors" and "stoics" are plural and do not agree with "anyone", which is singular.

Q20

Answer : C
  Category : Voice
Explanation

C) We need a reason why students would be "deeply shaken". The word "harsh" in choice C provides that reason.

Eliminate

A, B, D) No direct reason is given for why students would be deeply shaken.

Q21

Answer: B
Category: Punctuation
Explanation

B) The key to this question is recognizing the function of the list separated by commas. Notice that the list contains 4 elements (hands, chairs, shoulders, professors), and NOT 5 elements as one might incorrectly assume, because the word "highlights" after "and" is a verb, not a noun. The list of 4 is only separated by commas, without an "and" before the 4th element, which helps us recognize that the list is a side comment - not an integral part of the sentence. The cleanest way to set aside a comment is using dashes on either side of the list.

Eliminate

A, C, D) The list of 4 elements is not set aside effectively as a comment.

Q22

Answer: A
Category: Diction
Explanation

A) The underlined word must contrast with the unexpectedly barbaric behavior of these teachers who rip their students' music sheets. The word that provides the strongest contrast to "barbaric" is "prominent".

Eliminate

B, C, D) These words do not directly contrast with barbarism.

Q23

Answer: A
Category: Dashes
Explanation

A) A dash can function as the preposition "by". In this sentence, it explains how the wind shaped the planet. If we replace the dash with "by", we get a cohesive sentence: "Wind has shaped our planet by eroding, deflating, cooling, and dispersing".

Eliminate

B, C, D) A dash does not make sense here.

Q24

Answer: D
Category: Diction
Explanation

D) "Moreover" connects the one function of the wind (sculpting and moving) with the other (planting and pollinating).

Eliminate

A, B, C) None of these conjunctive adverbs are able to introduce an additional item to a list.

Q25

Answer: B
Category: Punctuation, Back Modifier
Explanation

B) The clause beginning with "where" is a dependent clause that modifies the word "world". Such back modifiers start with a comma right after the word they are modifying.

Eliminate

A, C, D) is either missing a comma after "world", or has an extraneous comma after "where".

Q26

Answer: C

Category: Idiom

Explanation

C) "from ... to ..." is an idiom that cannot be replaced by any other word.

Eliminate

A, B, D) replaces the word "to" in the idiom "from ... to ..." with another word.

Q27

Answer: A

Category: Insertion

Explanation

A) The topic sentence of the paragraph tells us that the wind is important to plant life. The sentence immediately preceding this point provides one example with seeds. Because the sentence immediately following this point introduces another function of the wind, if we do not add this sentence, there is only one example to support the topic sentence. Thus, inserting the sentence about pollen would help strengthen the main argument of this paragraph.

Eliminate

B) "key role of concentration of plants in wind dissemination" is backwards. It should be "key role of wind in dissemination of plants concentrated in one area".

C, D) We do need to insert this sentence to further support the main argument.

Q28

Answer: C

Category: Vocabulary

Explanation

C) The underlined portion must explain in what way animals depend on wind for survival. The word "warns" in choice C most clearly illustrates this dependency.

Eliminate

A, B, D) No word in these choices directly suggest dependency of animals on the wind for survival.

Q29

Answer: A

Category: Insertion, Content Order

Explanation

A) "however" suggests a contrast between the benefits and harms of the wind. Sentence 1 first mentions the harmful side of the wind after many previous sentences that describe its benefits, so this sentence should be inserted before sentence 1.

Eliminate

B, C, D) The harmful aspects of the wind already started to be discussed in sentence 1, so this given sentence must not come anywhere after sentence 1.

Q30

Answer: A

Category: Idiom

Explanation

A) "...to find out if ..." is an idiom that correctly illustrates why the elk sniffs the wind.

Eliminate

B, C, D) incorrectly give the reason why the elk sniffs the wind.

Q31

Answer : A
Category : Idiom
Explanation
   A) "vulnerable to" is the only acceptable idiom in the list of answers.
Eliminate
   B) While children may be taken to school, "feet … taken to cold winds" makes no sense.
   C) Nothing can be "attached to" wind.
   D) "freeze to cold winds" is idiomatically incorrect. The sentence should read "freeze due to cold winds".

Q32

Answer : A
Category : Graph Reading
Explanation
   A) The bar graphs are lower in Loess density with fewer trees present.
Eliminate
   B) No information is given on wind velocity.
   C) Since the amount of decrease is not consistent between the sets of adjacent bar graphs, proportionality cannot be determined.
   D) The amount of loess retained is not mentioned, so we cannot say it doubled, since we do not have a reference amount.

Q33

Answer : B
Category : Back Modifier
Explanation
   B) What follows the comma after "them" should be a dependent clause.
Eliminate
   A, C, D) These answer choices each contain a subject and a verb somewhere that makes them independent clauses.

Q34

Answer : C
Category : Pronoun Number Agreement
Explanation
   C) "Many fans" is plural, so only the possessive plural pronoun "their" fits here.
Eliminate
   A, B, D) these possessive pronouns are all singular, whereas the antecedent is plural.

Q35

Answer : D
Category : Insertion
Explanation
   D) The purists are mentioned solely as an example of fans who do not like film adaptations of their favorite books. The given sentence goes into too much detail about the purists that does not add any information to why they might not like their favorite books adapted on film.
Eliminate
   A, B) Adding this sentence will detract from the focus of the paragraph.
   C) Purists are mentioned before.

Q36

Answer: A
Category: Idiom
Explanation

A) "In a [adjective] way" is an idiom that describes how an action is performed. For example, we might say, "I looked at him in a secret way", which means I looked at him secretly. Only choice A is idiomatically correct.

Eliminate

B) capitalist excess is not tangible, so you cannot film something with it.
C) "it" suddenly introduces an unnecessary subject.
D) "capitalistic" is an adjective, which cannot describe a verb like "filming". To be considered an answer, choice D should read "excessively capitalistically".

Q37

Answer: C
Category: Idiom
Explanation

C) "See something as [V-ing] something else" is an idiom that requires the verb to end in -ing, and it means "to think that something is affecting something else". So "I do not see them as damaging the novel" means that the author does not think interpretations hurt a novel.

Eliminate

A, B, D) do not fit the idiomatic form.

Q38

Answer: A
Category: Diction
Explanation

A) "After all" means "without any expectations to the contrary", which means that what follows will continue the idea presented in the previous sentence. The current sentence alludes to *Twilight* as an example of a novel that was not damaged by creative interpretations, so "after all" is appropriate.

Eliminate

B, D) The example in this sentence is not contrary to the idea in the previous sentence.
C) Although "likewise" also can link two similar ideas, "after all" is more appropriate to the defiant tone of the author in this sentence's question.

Q39

Answer: D
Category: Verb Form
Explanation

D) The underlined portion is being used to modify the noun "work" like an adjective, so we need a gerund form "being disfigured" to describe that the work was disfigured.

Eliminate

A) This suggests that her work disfigured itself, which is wrong.
B, C) This suggests that her work disfigured something else, which is wrong.

Q40
Answer : C
Category : Replace
Explanation
C) What follows this sentence is a sentence that explains the difficulty of filmmakers in adating long novels to a short timespan. This is best summarized by the word "limitation" in choice C.
Eliminate
A, B, D) None of these choices contains a word that can effectively introduce the difficulty mentioned in the next sentence.

Q41
Answer : A
Category : Back Modifier
Explanation
A) A wh-word clause ensures that the task described in the first sentence is modified as "not an easy task" by the back modifier.
Eliminate
B) "and" does not adequately suggest the connection between the two sentences.
C, D) Using "not" right after the comma will result in modifying "hours", rather than modifying the task of showing a character's life.

Q42
Answer : C
Category : Diction
Explanation
C) The conjunctive adverb is used to contrast the complaint of fans with the successful result of a book. Choices B and C could both set up this contrast, but "while" more effectively sets up the ironic contrast of complaints versus success.
Eliminate
A, D) The fans' complaints are not the cause of success.
B) "Although" is not as effective at setting up an ironic contrast, because it does not have the sense of concurrency that "while" does.

Q43
Answer : D
Category : Delete/Replace
Explanation
D) The subject of the sentence is "fact" and verb is "makes". While "that literature is about interpretations" can serve as a relative clause describing "fact", the underlined portion serves no purpose. Deleting the underlined portion would be best.
Eliminate
A, B, C) Serves no grammatical purpose—it only interrupts the connection between the subject and the verb in this sentence.

Q44
Answer : D
Category : Tense Form
Explanation
D) Later in the sentence we can see "has left room for...", which means that this sentence requires "have + past participle" form of a verb.
Eliminate
A, B, C) These choices are not the "have + past participle" form of the verb "interpret".

Section 3. Math (Non-Calculator)

Q1

- **Linear Equations/Inequalities**

$\dfrac{(y+3)}{(y-4)} = 12$

$y+3 = 12y-48$

$11y = 51$

$y = \dfrac{51}{11}$

∴ Therefore, the answer is (D).

Q2

- **Functions**

$f(x) = \dfrac{x}{3} - 7$

$f(-6) = \dfrac{-6}{3} - 7$

$\quad = -2 - 7$

$\quad = -9$

∴ Therefore, the answer is (B).

Q3

- **Systems of Equation/Inequalities**

Given

$x - y = 2$,

$x = y + 2$.

Substitute for x in

$2x + 3y = 39$

$2(y+2) + 3y = 39$ to get

$2y + 4 + 3y = 39$

$5y = 35$

$y = 7$

$x = 9$

∴ Therefore, the answer is (B).

Q4

- **Linear Equations/Inequalities**

$\dfrac{c+2d}{c} = \dfrac{7}{16}$

$16(c+2d) = 7(c)$

$16c + 32d = 7c$

$9c + 32d = 0$

$9c = -32d$

$\dfrac{c}{d} = \dfrac{-32}{9}$

∴ Therefore, the answer is (D).

Q5

- **Equations**

$5(x^2 - 2x + 3) - 3(2x^2 - x + 4)$

$= 5x^2 - 10x + 15 - 6x^2 + 3x - 12$

$= -x^2 - 7x + 3$

$a = -1,\ b = -7$

$(-1)^2 - (-7) = 1 + 7 = 8$

∴ Therefore, the answer is (C).

Q6

- **Functions**

$f(x) = -2x^2 + 5x - c$

$2 = -2(0)^2 + 5(0) - c$

$c = -2$

$f(x) = -2x^2 + 5x + 2$

$f(1) = -2(1)^2 + 5(1) + 2$

$\quad = -2 + 5 + 2$

$\quad = 5$

∴ Therefore, the answer is (C).

Q7

• **Equation/Inequalities in Context**

$\dfrac{week}{2} \Rightarrow 4$

$\dfrac{week}{12} \Rightarrow 9$

From week 2 to week 12, the number of planks Harper has to chop increases by a total of 5. The total number of weeks from week 2 to week 12 is 10. Hence, Harper chops $\dfrac{5}{10}=0.5$ planks more every 1 week. This is equal to 1 planks more every 2 weeks.

∴ Therefore, the answer is (D).

Q8

• **Equations/Inequalities in the Coordinate Plane**
• **Absolute Value Advanced**

$|x| \geq 0 \longrightarrow |x|-2 \geq -2$
∴ Therefore, the answer is (D).

Q9

• **Equations**

$4a^4-12a^2b^3+9b^6$
Substitute: $2a^2=x$
$\qquad\qquad 3b^3=y$
$x^2-2xy+y^2$
$=(x-y)^2$
Plug in the original values back
$=(2a^2-3b^3)^2$
∴ Therefore, the answer is (A).

Q10

• **Linear Equations/Inequalities**

$\dfrac{k+3}{k-3}=18$

$k+3=18(k-3)$
$k+3=18k-54$
$17k=57$
$k=\dfrac{57}{17}$

∴ Therefore, the answer is (D).

Q11

• **Systems of Equation/Inequalities**

$y=3x-1$
$2xy=-x+1$
Plug $3x-1$ to y in the second equation
$2x(3x-1)=-x+1$
$6x^2-2x=-x+1$
$6x^2-x-1=0$
$(2x-1)(3x+1)=0$
$x=\dfrac{1}{2}$ or $-\dfrac{1}{3}$

Since $x>0$, $x=\dfrac{1}{2}$

$y=3\left(\dfrac{1}{2}\right)-1=\dfrac{1}{2}$

$x-y=\dfrac{1}{2}-\dfrac{1}{2}=0$

∴ Therefore, the answer is (C).

Q12

• **Equation/Inequalities in Context**

Each fire truck costs $12 and each train $17. Since the mother buys t trucks and $2f$ trains for her son,
Total cost $=12 \times t+17 \times 2f$
$\qquad\qquad =12t+34f$
∴ Therefore, the answer is (A).

Q13

• **Equations**

To remove i from the denominator, we need to use
$(a+b) \times (a-b) = a^2 - b^2$

$\dfrac{5i-15}{2+i}$

$= \dfrac{5i-15}{2+i} \times \dfrac{2-i}{2-i}$

$= \dfrac{(5i-15) \times (2-i)}{(2+i) \times (2-i)}$

$= \dfrac{10i - 30 - 5i^2 + 15i}{2^2 - i^2}$

$= \dfrac{10i - 30 - 5(-1) + 15i}{4 - (-1)}$

$= \dfrac{25i - 25}{5}$

$= -5 + 5i$

Therefore $a = -5$, $b = 5$
$a + b = 0$
∴ Therefore, the answer is (B).

Q14

• **Equations**

$2x^2 = p + \dfrac{q}{4}x$

$\Rightarrow 2x^2 - \dfrac{q}{4}x - p = 0$

Applying the quadratic formula,

$x = \dfrac{\dfrac{q}{4} \pm \sqrt{\left(-\dfrac{q}{4}\right)^2 - 4(2 \times -p)}}{4}$

$= \dfrac{\dfrac{q}{4} \pm \sqrt{\left(\dfrac{q^2}{16} + 8p\right)}}{4}$

$= \dfrac{q}{16} \pm \dfrac{\sqrt{\left(\dfrac{q^2}{16} + 8p\right)}}{4}$

∴ Therefore, the answer is (A).

Q15

• **Functions**

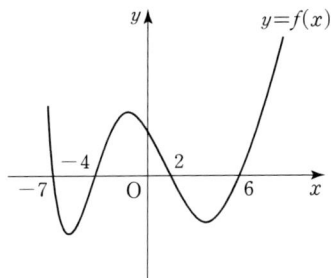

The x-intercepts of the graph are:
$x = -7, -4, 2, 6$
Therefore, $(x+7)$, $(x+4)$, $(x-2)$, and $(x-6)$ are factors of $f(x)$.
Put together,
$f(x) = (x+7)(x+4)(x-2)(x-6)$
∴ Therefore, the answer is (A).

Q16

• **Polygons**

$x = 180 - 140 = 40°$
∴ Therefore, the answer is 40.

Q17

• **Trigonometry**

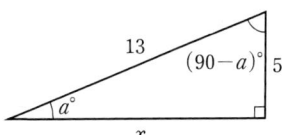

As given in the problem, $\sin a° = \dfrac{5}{13}$

$\sin a° = \cos(90-a)°$

$\cos(90-a)° = \dfrac{5}{13}$

∴ Therefore, the answer is $\dfrac{5}{13}$.

Q18

• **Equations**

$$\frac{12x^2+4x-5}{2x-3k}=6x+11+\frac{28}{2x-3k}$$

$12x^2+4x-5=(6x+11)(2x-3k)+28$
$12x^2+4x-5=12x^2+22x-18kx-33k+28$
$12x^2+4x-5=12x^2+(22-18k)x-33k+28$

Since the equation is true for all x,

$$\begin{cases} 4=22-18k \\ -5=-33k+28 \end{cases}$$

$$\begin{cases} 18k=18 \\ 33k=33 \end{cases}$$

$k=1$

∴ Therefore, the answer is 1.

Q19

• **Systems of Equations/Inequalities**

$\frac{x}{3}-y=\frac{4}{9}$ ⋯ $\boxed{\times 9}$

$\Rightarrow 3x-9y=4$ ⋯ $\boxed{\times 2}$

$\Rightarrow 6x-18y=8$ ⋯ ①

$3x+\frac{1}{2}y=6$ ⋯ $\boxed{\times 2}$

$\Rightarrow 6x+y=12$ ⋯ ②

①−②
$\Rightarrow -19y=-4$

$y=\frac{4}{19}$

∴ Therefore, the answer is $\frac{4}{19}$.

Q20

• **Equation/Inequalities in Context**

Let x=minutes past and y=number of words
When $x=0, y=50$
When $x=20, y=410$
Expressing this relationship with a graph,

Slope$=\frac{410-50}{20-0}=\frac{360}{20}=18$

$y=18x+50$

Insert $x=90$ into the above equation

$y=18(90)+50$
$\quad=1670$

After 90 minutes, Lee would have written 1670 words.

∴ Therefore, the answer is 1670.

Section 4. Math (Calculator)

Q1

• **Functions**

$f(-1) = -3$
$f(2) = 7$
$g(2) = -3$
$g(7) = -23$
$g(f(2)) = g(7)$
since $f(2) = 7$,
$g(7) = -23$
∴ Therefore, the answer is (D).

Q2

• **Equations**

$9x^2 + 9x - 28 = 0$
$(3x-4)(3x+7) = 0$
$x = \dfrac{4}{3}$ or $-\dfrac{7}{3}$

$p = \dfrac{4}{3}, \ q = -\dfrac{7}{3}$

$|p-q| = \left|\dfrac{4}{3} - \left(-\dfrac{7}{3}\right)\right|$

$= \left|\dfrac{4}{3} + \dfrac{7}{3}\right|$

$= \dfrac{11}{3}$

$3|p-q| = 3 \times \dfrac{11}{3} = 11$

∴ Therefore, the answer is (C).

Q3

• **Equation/Inequalities in Context**

I. True.
Let's assume Cooper received x dollars as allowance last summer.

Since $G = \dfrac{C}{3} + 4$, he would have gotten $\dfrac{x}{3} + 4$ points on his test.
Since he got an additional 3 dollars for his allowance this summer, it would mean he got $\dfrac{x+3}{3} + 4$ points on his test which is equal to $\dfrac{x}{3} + 5$.

Therefore, he got one more point on his grade than last year.

II. True.
$C = 3(G-4)$
$\quad = 3G - 12$
$C_2 = 3((G+12) - 4)$
$\quad = 3(G - 4 + 12)$
$\quad = 3G + 24$
$C_2 - C = (3G + 24) - (3G - 12)$
$\quad = 36$

III. False.
If we let C be the allowance last summer, and C_2 be the allowance this summer
$C = 3(G-4)$
$\quad = 3G - 12$
$C_2 = C - 1$
$\quad = 3(G-4) - 1$
$\quad = 3\left(G - 4 - \dfrac{1}{3}\right)$
$\quad = 3\left(\left(G - \dfrac{1}{3}\right) - 4\right)$

Cooper's grade decreased by only one third of a point.
∴ Therefore, the answer is (D).

Q4

• **Percentages**

Total $= 80$
Male $= 40$
Female $= 40$
Male OGL $= 40 \times 25\% = 10$
Female OGL $= 40 \times 30\% = 12$
$10 + 12 = 22$
∴ Therefore, the answer is (C).

Q5

• **Equation/Inequalities in Context**

$F = ma$
$2700 = m \cdot 300$
$m = 9$
∴ Therefore, the answer is (B).

Q6

• **Graphs and Data Analysis**
• **Probability**

14 is in the $11 \sim 15$ age range.
$11 \sim 15$ Total $= 962$
Number of people in the $11 \sim 15$ age group who prefer chocolate $= 462$
$\dfrac{462}{962} = \dfrac{231}{481}$

∴ Therefore, the answer is (A).

Q7

• **Graphs and Data Analysis**
• **Percentages**

Vanilla total $= 1214$
Total $= 3890$
$\dfrac{1214}{3890} = 31.2\%$

∴ Therefore, the answer is (C).

Q8

• **Coordinate Geometry**

$(0,0) \ (a,b)$
Slope $= \dfrac{b-0}{a-0} = \dfrac{b}{a}$

$y = \dfrac{b}{a} x$

$a + b = 0$ means that a and b have the same absolute value, but opposite signs.
$a \neq b$ means that a and b can't be 0.
∴ $\dfrac{b}{a} = \dfrac{-a}{a} = -1$

$y = -x \Rightarrow$ the slope is negative.
∴ Therefore, the answer is (B).

Q9

• **Graphs and Data Analysis**
• **Statistics**

Total hours $= 141$
Total students $= 20$
$\dfrac{141}{20} = 7.05$

mean $= 7.05$

$7.05 \times \dfrac{2}{5} = 2.82$

∴ Therefore, the answer is (A).

Q10

- **Percentages**
- **Graphs and Data Analysis**
- **Equation/Inequalities in Context**

Let x be the price of the ticket the three people bought. Then,
$3x + 6.89 + (3x - 20.98) = 45.85$
$6x + 6.89 - 20.98 = 45.85$
$6x + 6.89 = 66.83$
$6x = 59.94$
$x = 9.99$
3 people paid $9.99, so they are over 19.
1 person paid $6.89, so he/she is under 5.
1 person paid $8.99, so he/she is over 6, under 18.
Since 3 out of 5 family members are over 19,
$\frac{3}{5} = 60\%$

∴ Therefore, the answer is (B).

Q11

- **Graphs and Data Analysis**
- **Percentages**

Since only 1 person is in the category of over 6 and under 18, the price will only increase by:
$8.99 \times 0.1 = 0.899$
≈ 0.9

∴ Therefore, the answer is (A).

Q12

- **Equations**

$5x^2 - 15x + 6 = 0$
Using the quadratic formula,

$\frac{-(-15) \pm \sqrt{15^2 - 4(6)(5)}}{2(5)}$

$= \frac{15 \pm \sqrt{225 - 120}}{10}$

$= \frac{15}{10} \pm \frac{\sqrt{105}}{10}$

$\Rightarrow \frac{3}{2} + \frac{\sqrt{105}}{10}, \frac{3}{2} - \frac{\sqrt{105}}{10}$

are the two roots.

$\Rightarrow \frac{3}{2} + \frac{\sqrt{105}}{10} + \left(\frac{3}{2} - \frac{\sqrt{105}}{10}\right)$

is their sum.

$= \frac{3}{2} + \frac{\sqrt{105}}{10} + \frac{3}{2} - \frac{\sqrt{105}}{10}$

$= \frac{6}{2} = 3$

∴ Therefore, the answer is (D).

Q13

- **Percentages**

$w(x) = w \cdot \left(1 - \frac{2}{100}\right)^x$ where x equals number of months Jim has been on a diet. Therefore, after 10 months, Jim's weight will be:

$w(10) = 220\left(\frac{98}{100}\right)^{10}$

∴ Therefore, the answer is (C).

Q14

- **Circles**

If we set central angle AOB as θ,
$r = 6$
$6^2 \pi \cdot \dfrac{\theta}{360°} = 9\pi$

$36\pi \cdot \dfrac{\theta}{360°} = 9\pi$

$\dfrac{\theta}{360°} = \dfrac{9\pi}{36\pi} = \dfrac{1}{4}$

$\theta = 90° = \dfrac{\pi}{2}$

∴ Therefore, the answer is (B).

Q15

- **Graphs and Data Analysis**

34000 is the y-intercept of the graph, which means $y = 34000$ when $x = 0$.
Thus, 34000 represents the yearly wage that Andy received the first year of the job. (0 years passed)
∴ Therefore, the answer is (B).

Q16

- **Graphs and Data Analysis**
- **Linear Equations/Inequalities**

$y = 2000x + 34000$
$y = 2000(28) + 34000$
$ = 90000$
∴ Therefore, the answer is (D).

Q17

- **Circle Equation**

$x^2 + y^2 - 6x - 4y + 4 = 0$
$(x^2 - 6x) + (y^2 - 4y) + 4 = 0$
at this step we need to make perfect square equation for both x and y each. We do this by adding and subtracting the square of half of the coefficient for x and y.
$(x^2 - 6x + 9 - 9)$
$+$
$(y^2 - 4y + 4 - 4)$
$+$
4
$= 0$
$(x^2 - 6x + 9) + (y^2 - 4y + 4) + (-9) + (-4) + 4 = 0$
$(x-3)^2 + (y-2)^2 - 9 = 0$
$(x-3)^2 + (y-2)^2 = 9$
$(3, 2)$ is the center.
∴ Therefore, the answer is (A).

Q18

- **Rate**

1 mol dm^{-3} = 6 strips
1 strip = 8.25g
6 mol dm$^{-3} \left(\dfrac{6 \text{ strips}}{1 \text{ mol dm}^{-3}} \right) \left(\dfrac{8.25\text{g}}{1 \text{ strip}} \right) = 297\text{g}$

∴ Therefore, the answer is (A).

Q19

- **Rate**

$\dfrac{4800}{1600} = 3$

4800 years is equal to 3 cycles of half-life.
so, $x \times \dfrac{1}{2} \times \dfrac{1}{2} \times \dfrac{1}{2}$

$x \times \left(\dfrac{1}{2}\right)^3$

∴ Therefore, the answer is (B).

Q20

- **Functions**

$f(x) = 3x - 11$
$f(2x+1) = 3(2x+1) - 11$
$\qquad = 6x + 3 - 11$
$\qquad = 6x - 8$

∴ Therefore, the answer is (C).

Q21

- **Square Roots**
- **Equations**

$F = G \cdot \dfrac{m_1 m_2}{r^2}$

$r^2 F = G m_1 m_2$

$r^2 = \dfrac{G m_1 m_2}{F}$

$r = \sqrt{\dfrac{G m_1 m_2}{F}}$

∴ Therefore, the answer is (A).

Q22

- **Equations**
- **Ratio**

x meters apart $= F_x$

$F_x = \dfrac{G m_1 m_2}{x^2}$

y meters apart $= F_y$

$F_y = \dfrac{G m_1 m_2}{y^2}$

Since $F_x : F_y = 36 : 1$
and G, m_1, m_2 are common factors,

$\dfrac{1}{x^2} : \dfrac{1}{y^2} = 36 : 1$

$x^2 : y^2 = 1 : 36$

$x : y = 1 : 6$

∴ Therefore, the answer is (C).

Q23

- **Equations**
- **Factoring**

$3x^2 - 5x + 2 = 0$
$(x-1)(3x-2) = 0$
$x = 1$ or $\dfrac{2}{3}$

$1 \times \dfrac{2}{3} = \dfrac{2}{3}$

∴ Therefore, the answer is (C).

Q24

- **Equations**

$y = v_0 t - \dfrac{1}{2} g t^2$

$396.9 = 88.2 \cdot t - \dfrac{1}{2}(9.8) t^2$

$4.9 t^2 - 88.2 t + 396.9 = 0$
$t^2 - 18 t + 81 = 0$
$(t-9)(t-9) = 0$
$t = 9$

∴ Therefore, the answer is (C).

Q25

- **Equations**

$34.3 = v_0 \cdot 7 - \dfrac{1}{2}(9.8) \cdot (7^2)$

$34.3 = 7 v_0 - 240.1$
$7 v_0 = 274.4$
$v_0 = 39.2 \ m/s$

∴ Therefore, the answer is (D).

Q26

• **Polygons**

I. $w=y+z$
$y=z$
$w=2y$: True

II. $d=c+b$
$x=c,\ b=z$
$y=z=b$
$d=x+y$: True

III. $c=x$: Not true

IV. $b=z=y$: True

∴ Therefore, the answer is (C).

Q27

• **Systems of Equations/Inequalities**

Plug $x=2y+1$ into
$3xy=4y+5$ to get
$3(2y+1)y=4y+5$
$3(2y^2+y)=4y+5$
$6y^2+3y=4y+5$
$6y^2-y-5=0$
$(6y+5)(y-1)=0$
$y=-\dfrac{5}{6}$ or 1

Since $y>0$,
$y=1$
$x=2(1)+1=3$
$x-y=3-1=2$
∴ Therefore, the answer is (B).

Q28

• **Functions**
• **Graphs and Data Analysis**

Since $f(0)=1$,
A, B are not true.
C is true for $(0,\ 1)$
$\dfrac{0+2}{2}=1$

Check for another point $(2,\ 3)$
$\dfrac{2^2+2}{2}=\dfrac{6}{2}=3$

∴ Therefore, the answer is (C).

Q29

• **Linear Equations/Inequalities**

$10x-2=-10$
$10x=-8$
$x=-\dfrac{4}{5}$

$-20x-5=-20\left(-\dfrac{4}{5}\right)-5$
$=-4(-4)-5$
$=16-5$
$=11$

∴ Therefore, the answer is (C).

Q30

• **Linear Equations/Inequalities**

Plug $(72,\ 12)$ into $y=kx$ to get
$72k=12$
$k=\dfrac{12}{72}=\dfrac{1}{6}$

$y=\dfrac{1}{6}x$

$y=\dfrac{1}{6}(42)=7$

∴ Therefore, the answer is (C).

Q31

- **Graphs and Data Analysis**
- **Equations/Inequalities in the Coordinate Plane**

The phrase "above the line $y=x$" means that y exceeds x at a certain point.
Arugula and Watercress are the only 2 points which satisfy the condition above.
∴ Therefore, the answer is 2.

Q32

- **Graphs and Data Analysis**
- **Percentages**

Watercress price:
in 2013 ⟶ 11
in 2014 ⟶ 16
$\frac{16-11}{11} \times 100(\%) = 45.454545...(\%)$
∴ Therefore, the answer is 45.5(%)

Q33

- **Percentages**

Percentage of students with straight hair in Sean's class $=68.3\%$
Number of students expected to have straight hair in the lecture hall
$=315 \times 0.683$
$=215.145$
≈ 215
∴ Therefore, the answer is 215.

Q34

- **Graphs and Data Analysis**
- **Statistics**

$\frac{92+86+75+98+76}{5} = 85.4$

∴ Therefore, the answer is 85.4.

Q35

- **Graphs and Data Analysis**
- **Statistics**

mean 75 ⟶ Total score needed $=75 \times 5 = 375$
$77+83+67+71=298$
$375-298=77$
∴ Therefore, the answer is 77.

Q36

- **Equations/Inequalities in Context**

Let the depth and pressure of the beginning and end of the abyssal zone be two points on a coordinate plane:
$(13123, 5766)$ and $(19685, 8649)$
Then, let 1 unit $= 33$ feet
The number of units between the two coordinates is:
$\frac{19685-13123}{33} = 198.84$

Therefore, p equals the difference between the pressures at the beginning and end points divided by the number of units.
$p = \frac{8649-5766}{198.84} = 14.49909$
∴ Therefore, the answer is 14.5.

Q37

- **Graphs and Data Analysis**

Total $=41$
$41-14-9=18$
∴ Therefore, the answer is 18.

Q38

- **Graphs and Data Analysis**
- **Equations/Inequalities in Context**

Total number of students in Chemistry
$= 19 + 14 = 33$

$33 \times \dfrac{2}{3} = 22$ students take Biology

$22 - 9 = 13$ female students take Biology

Total female $= 13 + 19 + 14 = 46$

$46 + 41 = 87$

∴ Therefore, the answer is 87.

Part 4

Test Scoring

Scoring Your SAT Practice Test 1

성공적으로 SAT Practice Test를 마치셨습니다.
이제 아래 지침에 따라 점수환산을 해 보시기 바랍니다.

Scoring 개요

New SAT에서는 test score 뿐 아니라 cross-test score와 subscore가 계산되어 보고됩니다. Subscore 영역에서는 추가적인 진단결과를 학생을 비롯한 관련 기관으로 전송합니다. 더 자세한 내용은 http://collegereadiness.collegeboard.org/sat/scores 를 참고하시기 바랍니다.

준비물

Answer Sheet
Answer Key
Conversion Table

점수 계산

* SAT 총점 = Reading 점수 + Writing 점수 + Math 점수
* 각 영역별로 Raw Score(맞힌 문제 개수)를 세어 Conversion Table을 이용하여 점수를 환산
* 틀린 문제에 대한 감점 없음
  ① Section 1 Reading Test의 정답 개수를 세어 RAW SCORE 란에 기재한다.
  ② Conversion Table을 보고 RAW SCORE에 맞는 Reading Test Score를 찾는다.
  ③ Section 2 Writing and Language Test에서도 마찬가지로 정답 개수를 세어 기재한다.
  ④ Conversion Table을 보고 RAW SCORE에 맞는 Writing and Language Test Score를 찾는다.
  ⑤ 위의 두 Test Score를 합한 점수에 10을 곱한다. 이 점수는 Evidence-Based Reading and Writing Section score이다.
  ⑥ Section 3와 Section 4의 Math Test의 정답 개수를 세어 RAW SCORE 란에 기재한다.
  ⑦ Conversion Table을 보고 RAW SCORE에 맞는 Math Test Score를 찾는다.
  ⑧ 5번의 Evidence-Based Reading and Writing Section score와 Math Section score를 합한 점수가 SAT Practice Test의 총점이다. 점수대는 400~1600점대로 나온다.
  ⑨ Conversion Equation을 이용하면 편리하게 점수를 계산할 수 있다.

참고

* Subscore 및 Cross-test score는 실제 SAT 시험에서 Collegeboard가 자체적으로 평가하여 report하는 '부가분석' 자료이므로, 여기서는 다루지 않으니 참고하시기 바랍니다.
* 본 자료는 Collegeboard의 Scoring 자료를 바탕으로 한 것으로, 점수환산법, Conversion Table, Conversion Equation에 대한 저작권은 Collegeboard에 있습니다.

SAT Practice Test 1 Raw Score

<Answer Key>

Reading Test Answers

1 C	12 C	23 C	34 A	45 A
2 C	13 B	24 A	35 D	46 A
3 A	14 C	25 D	36 D	47 B
4 B	15 A	26 B	37 C	48 A
5 A	16 C	27 C	38 C	49 C
6 D	17 C	28 C	39 D	50 C
7 A	18 A	29 D	40 D	51 D
8 D	19 D	30 A	41 A	52 A
9 C	20 A	31 D	42 C	
10 D	21 D	32 D	43 B	
11 C	22 B	33 C	44 B	

READING TEST RAW SCORE
(NUMBER OF CORRECT ANSWERS)

Writing and Language Test Answers

1 C	12 B	23 A	34 C
2 A	13 C	24 D	35 D
3 C	14 B	25 B	36 A
4 B	15 D	26 C	37 C
5 D	16 C	27 A	38 A
6 A	17 D	28 C	39 D
7 B	18 B	29 A	40 C
8 C	19 D	30 A	41 A
9 C	20 C	31 A	42 C
10 A	21 B	32 A	43 D
11 B	22 A	33 B	44 D

WRITING AND LANGUAGE TEST RAW SCORE
(NUMBER OF CORRECT ANSWERS)

Math Test - No Calculator Answers

1 D	11 C
2 B	12 A
3 B	13 B
4 D	14 A
5 C	15 A
6 C	16 40
7 D	17 5/13
8 D	18 1
9 A	19 4/19
10 D	20 1670

MATH TEST NO CALCULATOR RAW SCORE
(NUMBER OF CORRECT ANSWERS)

Math Test - Calculator Answers

1 D	11 A	21 A	31 2
2 C	12 D	22 C	32 45.5
3 D	13 C	23 C	33 215
4 C	14 B	24 C	34 85.4
5 B	15 B	25 D	35 77
6 A	16 D	26 C	36 14.5
7 C	17 A	27 B	37 18
8 B	18 A	28 C	38 87
9 A	19 B	29 C	
10 B	20 C	30 C	

MATH TEST CALCULATOR RAW SCORE
(NUMBER OF CORRECT ANSWERS)

Raw Score Conversion Table (Section and Test Scores)

Raw Score (# Of Correct answers)	Math Section Score	Reading Test Score	Writing and Language Test Score	Raw Score (# Of Correct answers)	Math Section Score	Reading Test Score	Writing and Language Test Score
0	200	10	10	30	530	28	29
1	200	10	10	31	540	28	30
2	210	10	10	32	550	29	30
3	230	11	10	33	560	29	31
4	240	12	11	34	560	30	32
5	260	13	12	35	570	30	32
6	280	14	13	36	580	31	33
7	290	15	13	37	590	31	34
8	310	15	14	38	600	32	34
9	320	16	15	39	600	32	35
10	330	17	16	40	610	33	36
11	340	17	16	41	620	33	37
12	360	18	17	42	630	34	38
13	370	19	18	43	640	35	39
14	380	19	19	44	650	35	40
15	390	20	19	45	660	36	
16	410	21	20	46	670	37	
17	420	21	21	47	670	37	
18	430	22	21	48	680	38	
19	440	22	22	49	690	38	
20	450	23	23	50	700	39	
21	460	23	23	51	710	40	
22	470	24	24	52	730	40	
23	480	25	25	53	740		
24	480	25	25	54	750		
25	490	26	26	55	760		
26	500	26	26	56	780		
27	510	27	27	57	790		
28	520	28	28	58	800		
29	520	28	28				

Conversion Equation

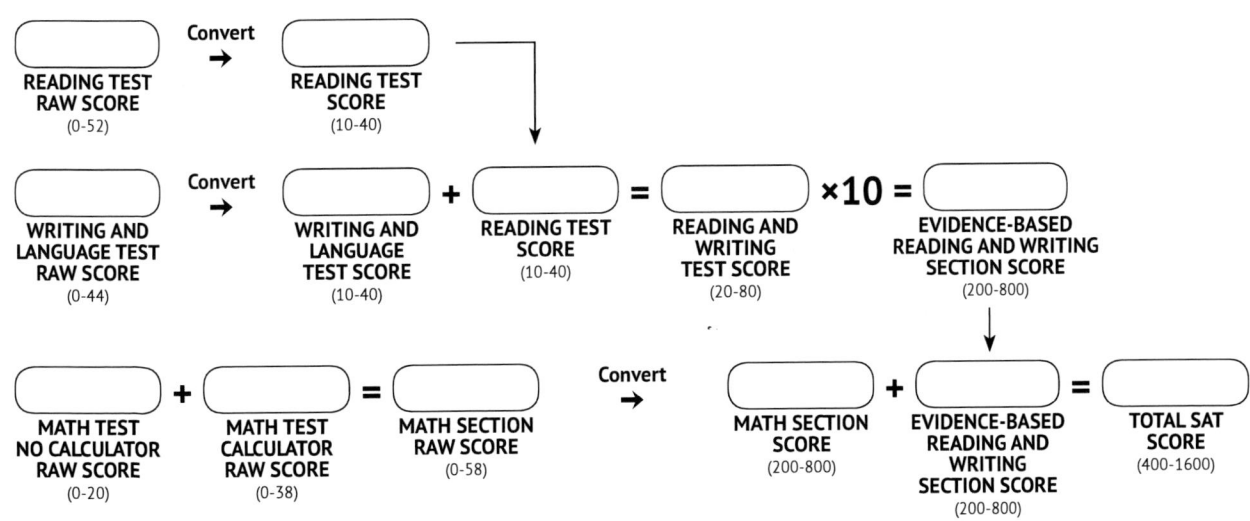

Paul's SAT® Practice Test 1

지은이   Paul Academy
발행인   김동현
발행처   엘티씨 (LTC)
출판등록   2008년 12월 24일
주　　소   서울특별시 성북구 북악산로 831
대표전화   02-558-2715
홈페이지   http://www.paulacademy.net
　　　　 http://blog.naver.com/paulacademy

ISBN 979-11-86461-05-1

※ 이 책은 엘티씨(LTC)가 저작권자와의 계약에 따라 발행한 것이므로 본사의 허락 없이는 어떠한 형태와 수단으로도 이 책의 내용을 이용하지 못합니다.

※ 잘못된 책은 구입하신 서점에서 바꾸어 드립니다.